The Phantom Friend

The Famous JUDY BOLTON *Mystery Stories*

By MARGARET SUTTON

In Order of Publication

THE VANISHING SHADOW
THE HAUNTED ATTIC
THE INVISIBLE CHIMES
SEVEN STRANGE CLUES
THE GHOST PARADE
THE YELLOW PHANTOM
THE MYSTIC BALL
THE VOICE IN THE SUITCASE
THE MYSTERIOUS HALF CAT
THE RIDDLE OF THE DOUBLE RING
THE UNFINISHED HOUSE
THE MIDNIGHT VISITOR
THE NAME ON THE BRACELET
THE CLUE IN THE PATCHWORK QUILT
THE MARK ON THE MIRROR
THE SECRET OF THE BARRED WINDOW
THE RAINBOW RIDDLE
THE LIVING PORTRAIT
THE SECRET OF THE MUSICAL TREE
THE WARNING ON THE WINDOW
THE CLUE OF THE STONE LANTERN
THE SPIRIT OF FOG ISLAND
THE BLACK CAT'S CLUE
THE FORBIDDEN CHEST
THE HAUNTED ROAD
THE CLUE IN THE RUINED CASTLE
THE TRAIL OF THE GREEN DOLL
THE HAUNTED FOUNTAIN
THE CLUE OF THE BROKEN WING
THE PHANTOM FRIEND

A JUDY BOLTON Mystery

The Phantom Friend

BY
Margaret Sutton

APPLEWOOD BOOKS
Bedford, Massachusetts

The Phantom Friend
was originally published in 1959.

Reprinted by permission of the estate of Margaret Sutton.
All Rights Reserved.

———•———

For a complete list of titles in the Judy Bolton Mysteries,
please visit judybolton.awb.com.

Thank you for purchasing an Applewood Book.
Applewood reprints America's lively classics—books from
the past that are still of interest to modern readers.
For a free copy of our current catalog, write to:

Applewood Books
P.O. Box 365
Bedford, MA 01730
www.awb.com

ISBN 978-1-4290-9050-6
Second Printing

MANUFACTURED IN THE U.S.A.

"The film will not be shown again!" Mr. Lenz said

A Judy Bolton Mystery

THE PHANTOM
FRIEND

By

Margaret Sutton

Grosset & Dunlap

PUBLISHERS   NEW YORK

The Phantom Friend

To
ALICE THORNE
Understanding Editor
and Real Friend

Contents

CHAPTER		PAGE
I	The Empty Chair	1
II	Clarissa Valentine	8
III	Tour Thirteen	15
IV	Strange Questions	22
V	Impossible Answers	30
VI	An Unfortunate Gift	37
VII	A Hidden Danger	43
VIII	The Witch's Curse	51
IX	Into the Mist	59
X	The Wrong Direction	66
XI	On the Train	73
XII	A Night of Terror	80
XIII	Before Daylight	88
XIV	Serious Trouble	94
XV	The Wrong Girl	101
XVI	The Name on the Calendar	107

x Contents

CHAPTER		PAGE
XVII	A Wanted Thief	113
XVIII	Thieves of the Mind	118
XIX	Uncovering the Facts	125
XX	Identified	130
XXI	Explained	136
XXII	Real Phantoms	143
XXIII	A Curious Letter	149
XXIV	Trapped!	155
XXV	Real Friends	161
XXVI	Talking Pillows	169

CHAPTER I

The Empty Chair

"I've had enough," exclaimed Irene Meredith, ducking to protect her face from a biting wind that was blowing across the skating area at Radio City. "Wouldn't you like to go inside now, Judy? It's really too cold to enjoy ice skating."

"It *is* cold," Judy agreed. "What a difference from the way it was in the summer! They had chairs out here then, and there were flowered umbrellas over the tables. But with the big Christmas tree up, Radio City is still beautiful in spite of the cold. Don't you wish—"

Judy did not finish the sentence.

"What's the matter with you two?" Pauline Faulkner demanded as she stopped short, almost colliding with Judy and Irene. "You can't just stop skating and gaze at the sights. Other people will bump into you. There, I knew it!"

"Watch it!" someone called out just too late.

Florence Garner, the fourth member of the skating party, turned sharply on her skates and went sprawling. But she was soon picking herself up.

"Are you hurt, Flo?" Irene asked solicitously.

"We're sorry," Judy added. "We didn't mean to upset you."

"I'm upset in more ways than one," Florence replied as the four girls skated off the ice. "Nothing is turning out the way I planned it. Pauline said—"

"Never mind what I said," Judy's dark-haired friend interrupted. "We'll discuss it at lunch."

Ten minutes later the rented skates had been returned, and the four girls were sitting around a table in a nearby restaurant. The waiter served steaming hot soup.

"This will warm us up," Irene commented over her soup plate. "Remember, Judy, I promised you we'd skate by the golden statue the next time you came to New York, and now we've done it."

"It was fun, but watching your television show will be the real treat," Judy told her. "When do you have to be at the studio for rehearsal?"

"Not until two. There's lots of time." Irene looked at the girl she had first known as Judy Bolton. She herself had been Irene Lang then, a timid little mill worker with a secret ambition to become a singer. Now, although her ambition had been realized and she was also a happy young wife and mother, she still looked to Judy for advice.

"I have a big decision to make," Irene confessed.

"If you were in my place, Judy, you'd know what to do. I don't want your little namesake to think of her mommy as one of the 'naughty' people on television. That's what she calls the people who do the commercials. We even have a little song we sing about it. Dale and I made it up to amuse little Judy. Of course, I'd never dare use it on my show," Irene added with a laugh. "The sponsor would never get over it."

"Sing it, Irene," Judy urged her.

"Right here?" The Golden Girl of TV and radio looked about the restaurant as if she had been asked to commit a crime. "I couldn't!"

"You could if you sang it very softly. Come on, I'd like to hear it, too," Pauline urged.

"Oh, very well," Irene gave in. "We call it '*When I Grow Up*,' and it goes like this:

"When I grow up I'll be a teacher or a hostess on a plane,
Or perhaps I'll be the weather girl and know about the rain.
I might sing and play like Mommy on TV or radio,
But I wouldn't do commercials,
No, I wouldn't do commercials,
No, I wouldn't do commercials and interrupt the show."

"I don't like them much either," agreed Judy after the song was over and she had stopped laughing. "Especially when you see the same thing over and over. It makes a person wonder—"

"Wonder what?" asked Pauline.

Irene laughed. "Judy is always wondering about something," she explained to Florence Garner. "Her husband, Peter Dobbs, calls her his wonder girl. Peter is—" She paused. "Shall I tell her, Judy?"

"She'll find out anyway. He's an FBI agent. It isn't something you can keep from your friends. Of course," Judy added, "there are times when it's better if people don't know."

"Criminals, you mean?"

"I mean anybody. Right now Peter is away on an assignment. I don't even know where he is. But let's talk about you, Flo," Judy suggested to change the subject. "Is it all right if I call you by your first name?"

"Of course. I know we just met today, but I feel as if I'd known you always," the brown-haired girl returned warmly. "Pauline has told me so much about you. I work for an advertising agency on Madison Avenue not far from the office where Emily Grimshaw holds forth."

Judy laughed. Pauline's employer was a literary agent who peddled the works of busy authors like Irene's husband, the detective story writer, Dale Meredith.

"She knows how to get contracts from publishers. Getting advertising accounts isn't easy, either," Florence continued. "I'm afraid a good many people share Irene's feelings about commercials and with reason. You should hear those ad men when they're in conference."

"I've read about them," declared Judy. "Is it true that advertising agencies employ psychologists to probe into people's minds and find out how to make them buy certain products?"

"Of course it's true." Pauline, the daughter of a psychiatrist, was indignant about it and said so.

"I don't see any harm in that," Flo said defensively. "They push the items they're paid to put across. Take the golden hair wash people, for instance. It was pure inspiration when they thought of Irene to sponsor their product. Golden Girl—golden hair wash! Can't you just see it on the TV screen? Their hair wash will sell like crazy—"

"And every girl will be a golden girl. I just can't agree to it," Irene interrupted. "I'd have to say I use the stuff when I don't. My hair is naturally this color."

"Mine is naturally this color, too. So help me!" put in Judy. "I dyed it once to disguise myself, but never again! Anyway, Peter likes redheads."

Pauline, a blue-eyed, black-haired beauty, seemed to be studying the others at the table. Each girl had her own distinctive coloring. Irene, with her naturally golden blond hair, wore it in a short bob. "To keep little Judy from pulling it when we romp," she said.

Judy wore her curly auburn hair in a long bob, while Florence Garner had her brown hair pinned high on her head. It, too, was curly and would have hung in ringlets if she had let it loose.

A fifth chair at the table was vacant. But Judy, suddenly a little homesick, could imagine Peter's sister sitting there to complete the picture.

"Honey's hair is darker than yours, Irene," she spoke up unexpectedly. "I call it honey colored. I hope she never uses that golden hair wash to change it. Honey simply wouldn't be Honey without her lovely honey-colored hair."

"Beauty is in the eye of the beholder," Pauline quoted airily. "Honey's hair is actually just plain dark blond."

"Our advertising will be directed toward dark blonds. Naturally they want their hair to be golden. Who is Honey, anyway?" asked Flo. "You keep looking at that empty chair as if she were sitting at the table with us."

"She is—in spirit." This was Irene. Judy laughed and added, "Honey is Peter's sister. We all love her, especially my brother, Horace. He's a newspaper reporter, and she's supplied him with plenty of news. There was a time when we didn't know she existed—"

"No wonder!" exclaimed Flo, laughing. "She's invisible now."

"Judy is trying to tell you about one of the mysteries she solved," Pauline explained, "but it's no use, Judy. There have been so many. Phantoms just follow you around waiting for you to pull off their sheets and show them up for what they are."

"And what are they?" asked Florence.

"Illusions, usually." Judy found the word a little difficult to define. "People think they see things that are really something quite different. Or else they're imaginary—"

"Like our phantom friend in the chair," Irene interrupted with a laugh. "Shall we ask the waiter to bring an extra order—"

"Are you expecting someone else to join you for lunch?" the waiter paused at the table to ask.

He had overheard only part of the conversation. Judy could hardly stop herself from laughing. She was about to tell him it was only a joke when a commotion at the cashier's desk drew her attention.

"I gave you a twenty-dollar bill," a tall girl with a country twang in her voice was insisting. "I know it was a twenty. But you've given me change for only a dollar. Where's the other nineteen dollars?"

CHAPTER II

Clarissa Valentine

"Isn't that the girl who was sitting alone at the next table?" asked Judy. "I noticed her watching you and smiling when you were singing that song, Irene. She seemed to be enjoying it."

"I knew I shouldn't—"

Irene stopped. The girl at the cashier's desk was really in trouble. Her voice had risen to a wail.

"You're a thief!" she cried out melodramatically. "Daddy warned me against people like you."

"Your daddy should have warned you to be more careful of your money," the cashier retorted sarcastically. "If you've lost twenty dollars—"

"I didn't lose it," she insisted. "You took it from me!"

"Poor girl! She really thinks she's been cheated," Irene whispered.

"She's beautiful," said Flo, "especially when she's angry. That girl ought to be in advertising. She's just the unspoiled type of beauty we're looking for. Of course, she ought to do something about her hair."

"Shampoo it with golden hair wash, I suppose? Please, Flo, don't try to make her over," Irene pleaded. "She's in enough trouble as it is."

"It looks as if the cashier is going to win the argument," observed Judy. "I feel sorry for the girl if he really is trying to cheat her."

"More likely she's trying to cheat him. She could be putting on an act," declared Pauline. "There, I told you so. Now she's turned on the tears."

In a moment the weeping country girl was surrounded by a little knot of concerned people who had left their tables to try and settle the matter. As they pressed toward him the cashier flung open the cash drawer.

"You see!" he pointed out. "There's no twenty! I haven't changed a twenty-dollar bill all day. She's made a mistake—"

"I did not," the girl retorted tearfully. "I know what I gave you. It was a twenty. Now I don't have money enough for my fare home."

"Where do you live?" he asked as if concerned.

"If I tell you, will you give me my nineteen dollars?"

"No!" he snapped. "You can't get away with a trick like that."

"Then I'll call the police," she threatened. "I won't let you cheat me out of all the money I have."

"Do you think the police will believe you?" the man inquired in a lower tone.

"I don't know!" cried the girl. "I don't know what happened to my twenty dollars if I didn't give it to you."

"There!" he exclaimed triumphantly. "You've admitted you lost it before you came into this restaurant."

"I did nothing of the kind. Doesn't anybody in New York care about the truth?" The girl seemed to be asking this question of the other people in the restaurant. "Please, mister," she began to plead, "give me back my change so I can go home."

"I'm sorry." The cashier seemed almost sympathetic. Yet he remained firm in his refusal to give the girl any money, insisting that she must have lost the bill she thought she gave him.

"Come, sit with us and tell us all about it." Judy offered on impulse. "We care about the truth."

"Then you'll look in that man's pockets," declared the nearly hysterical girl. "He took it—"

"We would report him to the manager," Florence Garner suggested.

"And make him lose his job? Mistakes happen," declared Pauline Faulkner. "We have no way of knowing which of you is in the right."

"That's true." The girl controlled her sobs and said, "It's kind of you to take an interest in me. I needed that twenty—"

"If we each chip in five dollars, you'll still have

money enough to take you home. You may consider it a loan," Irene said.

"Thanks." The girl smiled for the first time. "You're a genuine Golden Girl. I've seen you on television. I recognized your voice, too, when you sang that funny song. You're Irene Meredith!"

"Indeed I am." Irene introduced the other girls and offered the newcomer the vacant chair at the table.

"Now our phantom friend is real," declared Judy.

The girl looked startled. "I hope I'm real. Once," she confessed, "I looked in the mirror, and there was no reflection. It scared me half out of my wits. Why do you call me a phantom friend?"

"We were pretending we had a fifth girl at the table. It was just a joke. You do have a name, don't you?" Judy asked.

"It's Clarissa," the girl replied. "Clarissa Valentine."

"That sounds like a stage name," declared Pauline. "You aren't an actress, are you?"

"No, but I'd like to be. That's why I came to New York," Clarissa admitted. "At home we had a little theater group for a while. But they're old-fashioned down there. Some of the people in my father's parish didn't think it proper for a minister's daughter to act on the stage. We had to give up the little theater, so I coaxed Daddy to let me come here. I thought I could get a little part on TV, but I was wrong. I couldn't get any kind of a job. I was all out of money when Daddy sent me that twenty dollars for Christmas. He said he hoped I'd spend it for a ticket back home to

West Virginia. I was going to take the train tonight."

"You can still take it if you let us help you. Meantime," Florence Garner suggested, "why don't you join us for a tour of Radio City, my treat?"

"Do you mean it?" asked Clarissa, obviously surprised. "Touring Radio City was one of the things I especially wanted to do. Will we see ourselves on television?"

"We certainly will."

"Are you joking?" asked Judy. "How could we—"

"You'll see," Irene promised. "There's a live show you may catch if you hurry. But perhaps you'd rather wait and see mine tonight. Francine Dow is playing the Sleeping Beauty. You'll love her in it. I'm lucky to have her as a guest on my show. She can really act."

"So can you, Irene."

The Golden Girl of TV and radio tossed Judy's compliment aside. "I can sing and tell stories. That's about all. A part like this takes real talent. When you see the show you'll understand. Notice the equipment and don't be afraid to ask questions of the guide while you're taking the tour," Irene continued. "You'll enjoy my show more if you know the types of cameras being used and understand what the men on the floor are doing."

"Who are the men on the floor?" asked Clarissa.

"I haven't time to tell you now. The guide will explain it. I must dash, or I'll be late for rehearsal. Our studio is way uptown. Here's the address." Irene handed Judy a card on which she had written, "Admit four." "That includes Clarissa if she wants to come.

You know I'm not on one of the big networks."

"You could be," Florence began.

"Please," Irene stopped her. "I won't be on anything if I'm late for rehearsal. Turn in your contributions, girls, and let's go."

Clarissa seemed almost too eager to accept the four bills the girls offered her. They paid the cashier, counting their change carefully, and left the restaurant together.

Outside, the wind had increased, sending swirls and flurries of snow ahead of them as they crossed the street. They could scarcely see each other through the whiteness in the air.

"I'll leave you here. Cheer up, Flo. I'll let you know my decision in a day or two," Irene promised as she hurried off.

"Talk her into it, Judy," urged Pauline.

The four girls had entered the RCA Building, glad of the warmth they found inside.

"Talk her into *what?*" asked Judy. "I'm afraid I don't know the language. Do you have a new sponsor for Irene?"

"Yes, the golden hair wash people."

"Oh," Judy said and was suddenly silent.

"Would she be on one of the big networks?" asked Clarissa.

"Yes, the biggest. You'd see her on your TV at home, Judy. Isn't that worth thinking about? You can talk her into it if anyone can," Flo urged.

"I'll discuss it with her. How do the rest of you feel about it?" asked Judy.

"I think she ought to accept the offer," Pauline volunteered. "There's nothing wrong with commercials if they're in good taste. Lots of stars do them."

"It's a selling job like any other. The sponsor pays for the program," put in Flo. "I wish Irene could see it that way. She could sell golden hair wash."

"She doesn't believe in it," Judy objected. "If she used the stuff herself it would be different."

"I'd use it. I'd do anything," declared Clarissa. "I'd dye my hair green to get on TV."

"That's hardly ever necessary," laughed Flo.

"Do we really see ourselves on television when we take this tour?" Pauline questioned.

"I think so."

Judy asked at the information desk to make sure and came back all excited. "It's true!" she exclaimed. "The guide just told me."

"Then what are we waiting for?" asked Clarissa.

Taking Judy's arm, she pulled her on down the concourse until they came to a high desk where tickets were being sold. Judy found herself paying for them although Florence Garner had been the one to suggest the tour.

Clarissa clutched her ticket eagerly and whispered, as if to herself, "I hope I *show*. It would be terrible if I just faded away."

CHAPTER III

Tour Thirteen

"Did you say *faded* or *fainted?*" asked Judy. "People don't faint away unless they're ill. You feel all right, don't you?"

"Just a little trembly," Clarissa confessed. "I'm excited, I guess—"

"There's nothing to be excited about," Pauline told her. "I've taken this tour before. You just see behind the scenes in the different studios. It's a little dull, really."

Apparently Clarissa did not think so.

"Dull? How can you say that? If we see ourselves on television—"

A voice from a loudspeaker interrupted.

"Tour Thirteen leaves in five minutes."

"That must be us!" exclaimed Judy.

About a dozen people were waiting at the top of a

short flight of stairs. Some of them were watching TV as they waited. Judy and her friends joined them. The set had been tuned to one of the local channels.

"It's Teen Time Party!" exclaimed Pauline. "Wouldn't you like to be there dancing?"

"They're high school students, aren't they?" asked Judy.

"Most of them, I guess. There are probably a few professionals among them," Pauline added. "This one, for instance."

A lovely, golden-haired girl and her partner were caught by the camera in a close-up. The announcer turned to the audience and said, "Isn't her hair beautiful? You, too, can be a beautiful golden blonde. Shampoo glamorous new beauty into your hair with golden hair wash."

"I use it. Why don't you try it?" asked the girl on the television screen.

In a moment she was dancing again, mixing with the other teenagers as if she were one of them. She wasn't a star. Judy had never seen her on television before.

"This," she was thinking, "is all Irene would have to say. '*I use it.*' Three little words, but they're not true. Irene doesn't use it. Maybe she should. Her hair is dull and drab. Why am I thinking that?" Judy asked herself. "It's *my* hair that's dull and drab."

"Yours?" Florence asked. Judy had not realized she was speaking her thoughts aloud. Florence went on, "That's funny, Judy. You wouldn't want your hair any brighter than it is."

"No," Judy admitted, "I guess I wouldn't. I always thought it was too bright before. I don't know why I said that."

"I do," Clarissa spoke up. "You read my thoughts. I was just thinking my hair is dull. I could be beautiful if I didn't have this drab, dull hair. It was lighter when I was small. It was really golden then. But all at once it began to get darker. I changed in other ways, too. Mother says I must be a changeling—"

"Changelings aren't real," Pauline stopped her. "They're what witches were supposed to leave when they snatched real children."

"There's a witch in Sleeping Beauty," Flo put in. "Irene says her dance is the best thing in the whole show. This tour is nothing compared to what we'll see tonight, but it will kill time until seven o'clock."

"You mean six-thirty," Judy corrected her. "We have to be at the studio half an hour before the show begins, and I would like to be there even earlier than that so Irene can explain things. There's so much I don't know."

The guide, overhearing Judy's remark, smiled and said, "So you're going to visit the Golden Girl show?"

"It's treason," Pauline whispered. "Irene's show is on another channel. So is Teen Time Party. One of the tourists must have turned it on."

It was off now. In its place a gay crowd of young people were singing the praises of a popular cigarette.

"That's one of our accounts," Flo said proudly.

"It's wasted on me. I don't smoke," laughed Judy as the tour moved on to a large room lined with pictures of television stars appearing on the big network. People were pointing and exclaiming, each one seeming to have his own favorite.

"Irene's picture should be up there," Flo remarked, "but she wouldn't do commercials, no, she wouldn't do commercials, no, she *wouldn't* do commercials—"

"Please, Flo, don't make fun of Irene," begged Judy. "She's only standing up for what she believes is the right thing."

"How right is it to throw away money you could be making?" Flo countered. "Judy, you must talk her into accepting this offer. Tell her you think it's right."

"I'm not sure what I think. If she really used golden hair wash then she wouldn't have to say anything that wasn't true, would she? I think I'll buy a bottle and ask her to try it," Judy decided.

"Should I try it, too? Brown is a dull color," Flo began, but was interrupted. The guide, a brown-haired girl herself, stepped to the head of the line and announced that the tour was about to begin. The group followed her to an elevator that whisked them up to one of the smaller studios. They had just missed the show Irene had mentioned.

"Would you like to watch a set being dismantled? There aren't any live shows being televised at present," the guide said as she ushered the group to a row of seats behind what she told them was soundproof glass. A small television set that she called a monitor was at the left of the seats. In front of it, on the other side of the glass, the studio floor was alive with activity. Cameras and microphones were being pushed out of the way. The walls of what had been an indoor scene were rolled back and replaced by a huge weather map. The weather girl would be the next person to use this studio.

"Will we see her?" asked Judy.

This was a program she and Peter often watched at their home in Dry Brook Hollow. She thought of watching Irene, and the wish to see her dearest friend on television became so strong she could think of nothing else except, "She should use golden hair wash."

"Judy! We're going to the control room now."

Judy came out of her trance to realize that Pauline was speaking to her. She was the last one on the line that wended its way toward the glass-enclosed control room where the engineers sat before rows of monitor screens awaiting word from the director.

"He says 'take one' or 'take two,' and in a split second the picture he wants is on the screen," the guide explained. "When a live show is on the air, the cameras are working all the time."

"What about the lights?" asked one of the strangers taking the tour.

"Lighting a show is an engineering feat in itself." And the guide went on to explain the flashing red and greeen lights as well as the other technical equipment being handled by the crew on duty in the control room. On the wall above their heads were clocks that told what time it was all over the world.

"Wonderful, isn't it?" everyone agreed.

A wall chart farther down the corridor explained

the inside story of color television. It was complete with push buttons and flashing lights. The men taking the tour were especially interested. Pauline said she recognized one of them.

"I recognize him, too," Florence agreed. "He works for our agency. It's funny he didn't speak to me."

"He's too interested in what the guide is telling him to speak to anybody," Judy observed.

The man was interested. He was young with straight brown hair that kept falling over his forehead as he leaned forward to examine this or that gadget. The guide was giving him most of her attention.

"When do we see ourselves on TV?" Clarissa whispered.

"Patience," Pauline told her. "We're coming to that. We stand in front of a camera, and the guide interviews us, but I think we go up to the sound-effects room first."

"That's radio, isn't it? I watched the sound-effects man once on a radio broadcast," Judy remembered. "It was right here in Radio City, but I had a mystery to solve and didn't take the whole tour."

The others asked her about the mystery, and she began to tell them about what happened before she and Peter Dobbs were married. "Irene had a radio show then. It was the summer before little Judy was born. Honey was just out of art school. Peter and I drove to New York to bring her home."

"Who is Honey?" asked Clarissa.

For the second time that day Judy explained that

Peter's sister had been in their thoughts when they pretended at the table in the restaurant. "We called her a phantom just for fun. And then you came and sat in her chair," Judy continued. "It did seem a little weird. You're like Honey in many ways. You're taller, of course, and your hair is darker—"

"It won't be much longer," declared Clarissa. "I'm going to buy a bottle of that golden hair wash with some of the money you girls lent me. Then I'll be beautiful."

"You *are* beautiful," Flo insisted. "Didn't I say so, girls? There's nothing wrong with the color of your hair."

"It's drab. It's dull."

"Oh, stop it, Clarissa!" cried Judy. "We lent you that money for your fare home, not to waste on shampoo."

"It won't be wasted. You'll see."

"What will your folks say?" asked Pauline. "You're the daughter of a country minister, aren't you? People will talk—"

"Let them! I won't care if I'm beautiful."

"You're impossible!" Flo exclaimed. "How old are you, anyway? You ought to be at home going to school."

Clarissa wouldn't tell her age. She wouldn't tell anything more about herself or her plans. Judy was looking forward to the TV interviews. The guide might ask Clarissa some leading questions.

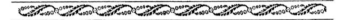

CHAPTER IV

Strange Questions

"We're supposed to be finding out things on this tour," complained Judy as they stopped to look in on another studio, "but I keep thinking about my hair. I'm like you, Clarissa. I want to rush right out and buy a bottle of that golden hair wash. But why? I'd never use it."

"Maybe you want to buy it for Irene," Flo suggested.

"I don't really. That's just it. I don't want to buy it at all, and yet I feel compelled to try it. Why?"

"I know why I want to," Clarissa insisted. "If I had beautiful golden hair I might not go home at all. I might stay here and get a job doing commercials. See that girl on the floor now? I could do what she's doing. I could demonstrate a magic cleaner as well as she can. I did plenty of cleaning and scrubbing at home, and I didn't have any little fairy to help me, either. Look, girls! See that little fairy dancing around the sink. It isn't there, but you can see it on the monitor. How do they make it look like that?"

The guide explained it. A cartoon film was placed in a camera she called a balopticon so that the fairy appeared to be helping the girl clean the sink, dancing about in the powder and waving her magic wand. Little specks of stardust seemed to fly from the end of it until the whole kitchen was spotless.

"Interesting, isn't it?" she finished.

Some of the people found it so. Questions were asked about the properties set up to make the studio look like a kitchen. The floor was a design of squares painted on with water colors. It would be washed away when the set was changed.

Others were beginning to act bored. Judy noticed several women stopping to take mirrors out of their purses and look at themselves critically. One of them asked, "Will we need stage makeup? I've heard the stars use plenty of it."

"Not at all," replied the guide. "We will appear as we are."

"Oh dear!" wailed Clarissa. "I look terrible. My hair is dull. My hair is drab—"

"Turn her off, somebody!" Pauline interrupted. "We've heard that record before."

"She has my head spinning like a record," declared Judy. "I hope I remember some of the things we've learned on this tour. A balopticon is one kind of camera and a dolly is another—"

"It isn't the camera. It's the truck that's called a dolly," Pauline corrected her. "You see, it takes two men to work it. That's the camera man up there on the funny little seat."

"Why is he wearing earphones? Did the guide say?"

"She did say something about the men on the studio floor hearing directions from the control room. It is complicated," put in Flo. "You can't be expected to remember most of it."

"Well, anyway, I know that big fishing-line thing is the mike boom. If I remember that much, Irene won't think I'm too ignorant," Judy concluded. "I wonder how they keep all that equipment from showing on a live TV show."

The guide took time to explain it, telling them how accurately the cameras had to be focused so that the mike boom which dangled its microphone right over the heads of the performers was always just out of the picture.

"It does look like a fishing line, doesn't it?" she agreed. "Are there any more questions before we go up to the sound room?"

Clarissa started to ask something and then changed her mind, saying, "It doesn't matter."

The guide gave a little performance of her own to demonstrate the sound effects. Rain was rice falling on waxed paper. Fire was the crackle of cellophane. There were blocks of wood for marching soldiers and other sounds equally amazing.

"And now," she announced, emerging from the

glassed-in sound room, "we are ready to see our-selves on television."

A little ripple of anticipation went down the line that now followed the uniformed guide to another studio containing a pedestal camera and a television set.

"It's a closed circuit," she explained. "Your friends at home won't see you, but you will see yourselves and each other. You will each have a chance to say a few words—"

"What will we say?" Clarissa inquired.

"I'll ask you questions. You just answer them. Most of you are from out of town, I presume. People taking these tours usually are. You, sir?" She spoke to a tall gentleman with a thick mustache. "Step up here before the camera and tell us a little about yourself. Can you see yourself on the screen?"

He smiled, showing white teeth that looked even whiter as his face was framed in the TV set.

"I see. I look good. I am here from Rio de Janeiro on business."

The man talked about his business which was manu-facturing plastic caps. It was hard to understand him because of his accent. The others taking the tour waited their turns, standing along a wall at the side of the room. As the line moved up, Clarissa became more and more nervous.

"I may not show," she kept insisting.

"Of course you'll show," Judy reassured her. "You see how clear the picture is. Everybody else shows."

As the line moved up, Clarissa became more and
more nervous

"I didn't show in the mirror."

Pauline turned to her in surprise.

"Weren't you joking when you said that?" she asked.

"I was never more serious in my life," replied Clarissa. "It's the truth. Once I really did look in a mirror, and there was no reflection. I've been afraid of—of something ever since it happened. My brother noticed it first and said, 'Clar, you don't show!' He always calls me Clar. It rhymes with jar the way he says it. I thought he was teasing me, but then I looked, and sure enough, my face didn't show at all."

"Was the mirror broken?" asked Flo.

"No, it wasn't broken. I'm sure, because I noticed my brother looking in it afterwards, and his reflection was as plain as anything. My younger sisters looked, too. They saw themselves all right. There are six of us, including Mother and Daddy," Clarissa explained. "It was Mother's mirror. She still uses it. I was the only one who didn't show. Mother laughed and said I must be a changeling, but I didn't think it was funny. It still scares me. How could a thing like that happen?"

"There must be an explanation for it," Judy replied. Here was another mystery for her to solve. But, instead of concentrating on it, her thoughts kept returning to her hair. Would it look dull and drab on television?

The brown-haired man Pauline and Flo thought they knew stepped up before the camera and announced that he was from Hollywood.

"No wonder he didn't recognize me!" Flo exclaimed. "He isn't the young man who works in our office and yet he does look like him. Maybe he has a twin brother."

"Or a double. Lots of people have doubles—"

"No, Judy, only a few people have them," Pauline objected, and Judy had to agree with her. One of the wonderful things about people, she thought, was that no two of them were exactly alike. Even identical twins could be told apart by their fingerprints, and usually there were other important differences. Judy found herself watching for individual characteristics as, one by one, the people stepped before the camera. A photograph of skyscrapers on the backdrop behind them made it appear to be a sidewalk interview.

"Are you from out of town?" was the question most frequently asked by the guide.

Most of them were. Some came from as far away as Brazil or Switzerland. Two were from Texas, and two said they were from the state of Washington. When Judy replied that she lived in Pennsylvania she felt as if she were practically at home.

"Your hair looked lighter on TV," Flo told her when she stepped back in line.

"Did it?" asked Judy. "I kept worrying for fear it would look dark. I don't know why. Dark hair is pretty. I like the color of yours."

"I don't. It's drab—"

"Please," Judy stopped her. "You're next, Clarissa. What's the matter? Are you afraid to go up?"

"Yes," Clarissa admitted, suddenly all a-tremble. "I'm afraid—"

"Come on. Take a good look at yourself," advised Pauline, giving her a little push.

"All right. I'll do it."

Unwilling and still trembling, Clarissa stepped up before the camera. She stood in the exact spot where Judy had been standing. The guide began to ask questions.

"You're from West Virginia, aren't you? What town? Look into the camera and tell me—"

A long drawn-out wail from Clarissa interrupted her.

"I am looking," she cried, "but I don't see anything! What's the matter with me? Why don't I show?"

CHAPTER V

Impossible Answers

An exclamation went up from the people taking the tour. "She's right. There isn't any picture?"

"What's that bright spot of light?" asked Judy.

She had never seen anything like it before. The picture on the television screen seemed to be closing in on all sides. Instead of Clarissa's face, an eerie, wavering light danced before her eyes.

"There must be something wrong with the set," the guide began. "Step back a moment, and I'll see—"

She stopped. Clarissa's face had become waxy white. She would have fallen if Judy hadn't rushed to her side.

"It's all right," Judy said soothingly. "Some little technical thing probably went wrong—"

"No, Judy. It wasn't that. I am a phantom. I saw

myself the way I really am. Oh, help me!" wailed Clarissa as she slumped forward and slipped to the floor.

"I'm sorry," Judy gasped. "I tried to hold her."

"It's all right, Judy," Pauline told her. "You did save her from a hard fall."

"She's ill. We must get her to the first-aid station at once." The guide, obviously a little shaken herself, took charge. Two of the men carried Clarissa to a door with a red cross and the words: FIRST AID, lettered on it. Here she was left with an efficient, white-uniformed nurse who assured Judy that her friend would be all right, but that she must rest for half an hour.

"May we stay with her?" asked Flo. "I think she was frightened."

"In that case," replied the nurse, "it might be better for her to be alone until she's fully recovered from the shock. What happened? Was the guide in any way at fault?"

"No," Judy hastened to assure her. "In fact, she was very efficient. It was probably something technical. I don't understand the inside workings of television very well."

The nurse smiled. "Neither do I. The inside workings of the human mind are even more mysterious. This girl should see a doctor or a psychiatrist—"

"No-oo," came a sob from Clarissa.

The nurse quieted her, breaking a capsule for her to inhale. She asked the girl for her name and address, but all Clarissa said was, "I'm not real. I'll fade away altogether pretty soon. Please, just leave me alone."

"Perhaps that's best." Quietly the nurse escorted Judy, Pauline, and Flo into the next room where she began to ask questions.

"You say the girl's name is Clarissa Valentine?"

Judy nodded, and the nurse wrote it down.

"Where does she live?" was her next question.

The three girls looked at each other in bewilderment. "She said West Virginia, didn't she? We don't know the name of the town."

"It's all right. I'll get the rest of the information from her as soon as she's feeling better. Now," said the nurse, "if you will leave your names and tell me where I can reach you, I think it will be all right for you to go back and finish your tour. Give our patient half an hour, and I think I can convince her she isn't in any danger of fading away."

"We forgot to tell the nurse that Clarissa's father is a minister," Judy said suddenly when they were halfway down the hall.

"Maybe he isn't. I still think she's putting on an act," declared Pauline. "She's the sort that craves attention."

"How do you know what sort she is?" Flo asked. "She's practically a stranger."

"I was beginning to think of her as a friend," objected Judy. "Everybody craves attention in one way or another. If she's in trouble, isn't it up to us to help her?"

"We have helped her," Pauline reminded Judy. "We

each gave her five dollars, didn't we? I should think that was help enough."

"Maybe money isn't what she needs."

Flo laughed at that. "Isn't money what everybody needs? Quit dreaming, Judy. Why do you think all these people are rushing about like ants in an ant hill? If it isn't to get money, it's to spend it."

"It's more than that." Judy wanted to explain, but the right words wouldn't come. They had just entered the room where the closed circuit TV set was being viewed by the tourists.

"There's nothing wrong with it now," observed Pauline. "The picture is just as clear as ever. We'll bring Clarissa back here—"

"If she'll come."

Flo, who had not yet seen herself on TV, stepped up before the camera. She frowned at her image framed in the TV set against the background of tall buildings. The picture was clear.

"If you hadn't scowled at yourself you would have looked all right," Judy told her.

"But my hair looked dull—"

"That's Clarissa's complaint, not yours, Flo. I do believe she's hypnotized you into saying it," declared Pauline.

Judy wondered if that could be possible. Afterwards she wished she had asked the guide what went wrong with the picture when Clarissa fainted. For when they went back to get her she did refuse to come and see herself.

"Anyway," Clarissa added, "the tour is over, and I'm all right now. The nurse gave me some capsules to break and inhale if I feel faint during Irene's show."

"Maybe you shouldn't go," Pauline began.

"But you invited me—"

"Of course we did," Judy broke in. "Irene is expecting all four of us."

"You're so good to me!" exclaimed Clarissa. She glanced about the small room with its first-aid equipment as if in doubt about something. Then she said, "The nurse went out for a minute. We don't need to wait for her. Shall we go?"

Judy was glad to leave. There was something oppressive in the air. The closed-in cubicle was left for the next emergency patient. As soon as they were outside in the wintry air, the color came back to Clarissa's cheeks, and she appeared to be quite herself again. Swirls of snow were still blowing about, now hiding, now revealing the street ahead.

They stopped in a drugstore and had coffee and a quick sandwich. As they were about to leave, Judy remembered something.

"I was going to buy a bottle of golden hair wash!" she exclaimed.

"I was, too," Flo said. "This looks like as good a place as any."

"Golden hair wash," breathed Clarissa.

"Make it three bottles," Judy heard herself saying to the druggist.

He regarded her curiously.

"You aren't going to use that stuff on your red hair, are you?" he inquired.

"No," replied Judy, feeling uncomfortable under his puzzled gaze. "It's for a friend."

He shook his head. "I can't understand it. This is the thirteenth bottle I've sold in the last half hour. Ordinarily the stuff doesn't sell too well. You have to be careful how you use it. Follow the directions, and don't let any of it get into your eyes or your mouth. It will gradually change the color of your hair. Is that what you want?"

"It's what I want. I want to change everything about me," declared Clarissa.

Hugging her bottle of shampoo as if it were a magic potion, she followed the others out of the store.

"Now I'll be beautiful," she kept saying. "Now I'll be a golden girl too."

Flo agreed with her. "I'll have golden hair, too. It's bound to make me look better. Don't you think so, Judy?"

The wind blew harder. Judy could scarcely make herself heard above the weird whistling noise it was making.

"You won't be Flo," she shouted. "You'll look so different without your pretty, brown hair."

"Who will I be?" Flo asked, glancing at Clarissa just as the wind caught her scarf and sent it flapping. "Will people call me a changeling?"

"Now you're laughing at me," Clarissa charged. "Well, you can joke if you want to, but I still have a feeling I'm not real. You must have felt there was something different about me when you called me a phantom friend."

"We were talking about the empty chair," Judy began.

"People say things sometimes without knowing why they say them, and they turn out to be true," Clarissa insisted. "Mother didn't mean it when she called me a changeling, either, but she made me feel like one. You know—as if the real me is hidden somewhere under this dull, drab hair."

"Did your mother call it dull and drab?" asked Flo. "Is that why you've hypnotized the rest of us into buying this golden hair wash?"

"Me? Hypnotized you? I thought it was the other way around." Clarissa seemed genuinely distressed. She turned to look at Flo, and at that moment the thirteenth bottle of golden hair wash fell and broke, spilling all over the snow.

"Look what you made me do!" With a sound that was more of a sob than a laugh, Clarissa added, "Now I can never be a golden girl. I can never find the really, truly me!"

CHAPTER VI

An Unfortunate Gift

Judy acted on impulse. She thrust her own bottle of shampoo into Clarissa's gloved hand.

"Take it," she urged the surprised girl. "I don't know why I bought it in the first place. Irene doesn't need it. I'm sure she'd never use it. She'd probably think I was out of my mind to buy it for her."

"Take mine, too. I don't like the looks of the stuff when it's spilled. And I'd be afraid to use it after what that druggist said," declared Flo. "I wish—"

"Wait!" cried Clarissa before Flo could finish. "See what it does to me before you condemn it. I'll be a glamorous new person because of this shampoo. You just wait and see what happens to me!"

Fear seized Judy. Suddenly she was afraid of what would happen. Already she felt herself in the grip of something she could neither explain nor understand. Was Clarissa in its grip, too? The girl's mood had changed so suddenly it was alarming. Had the gift of two bottles of shampoo worked the transformation? Judy considered it unlikely.

"You've changed already. You don't need to change the color of your hair," she began.

"It's drab."

"No, it isn't, Clarissa. I don't know what makes you keep saying that. It's just your imagination."

The girl smiled impishly and tossed her head. A white scarf covered her hair except for a few stray wisps that were blowing in the wind. The ends of her scarf fluttered like white wings behind her.

"I do have an imagination," she admitted as if revealing a secret she had meant to keep. "Sometimes it plays tricks on me."

"That's what it was when you thought the cashier stole your twenty dollars," Pauline said. "You just imagined you gave it to him."

"Did I?" Clarissa seemed ready to admit it. "You don't suppose the wind could have picked the money out of my hand, do you? It's fierce today, isn't it? It wouldn't surprise me a bit if it picked me up and carried me away."

Judy laughed at that.

"I can just see you being swept up into the clouds with that white scarf trailing behind you. Like the witch who rides through the sky on Hallowe'en."

"She's the thirteenth fairy in Sleeping Beauty," replied Clarissa, and she was laughing, too. "It was always my favorite fairy tale. I can hardly wait to see Irene—"

"She isn't playing the part of Sleeping Beauty," Flo interrupted. "She just introduces the show and sings."

"I know. She told us. Sleeping Beauty is being played by a guest star, Francine Dow. I've seen her on television, and she's lovely. I wonder if she uses golden hair wash."

"Of course she doesn't. Her hair is dark," Flo said.

"No, it's light," Pauline contradicted.

Pauline and Flo were actually arguing about it.

"We'll see what color it is when we reach the studio," Judy told them, "not that it matters. I'm tired of all this talk about hair."

"How much farther is it?" asked Clarissa. "It seems to me we've been walking forever in this wind."

"We're there," announced Pauline as they rounded the next corner. "See the sign, GOLDEN GIRL SHOW. The theater looks a little sad, doesn't it? They've turned an old movie house into a TV studio."

Judy was eager to see how the cameras and other technical equipment were arranged inside the theater building.

"It's warm, thank goodness!" she exclaimed as they entered, showing their pass to a man in the lobby. He waved a tired hand toward the left side of the theater.

"You're early. Take any four seats," he said with an uninterested drawl.

"Don't we get a chance to see the dressing rooms?" Clarissa asked. "I've always wanted to see the dressing rooms of the stars."

"We'll see them afterwards, I guess. I wonder where the control room is. I think I'll look around and see if I can find it."

"Wait, Judy!" said Pauline. "I don't think we should go exploring."

But Judy didn't see any reason why she shouldn't leave her seat if the others saved it for her. She shook the snow from her coat and left it there so people would know the seat was taken.

Most of the folding seats had been removed from the theater to make room for the TV equipment. Those that remained were directly under the balcony. Judy hesitated a moment, looking around. Then she walked down the aisle between the rows of seats until she came to what was called the studio floor. Immediately she recognized the different kinds of cameras and microphones. The big mike boom, mounted on its three-wheeled platform, stood to one side. So did the dolly, its funny little up-in-the-air seat now empty. Judy gazed at it for a moment. Then she turned around. There on the balcony was the glass-enclosed control room with its monitors and flashing lights.

"I learned more than I thought I did on that tour," she told the others when she returned to her seat. "The control room is just over our heads on what used to be the balcony of the old theater. There's a movie on this channel now."

"We've been watching it. Probably it's being shown for the second time in this theatre," Pauline said. "It's so ancient I'm sure it must have been one of the pictures shown here before this building was made over into a TV studio." She pointed. "See it! They have another one of those monitors suspended from a beam just over the middle aisle."

"That's wonderful!" exclaimed Judy. "We can watch Irene's show on TV at the same time we're seeing it on the stage. Oh, there she is!"

Judy broke off with this exclamation as the people in the surrounding seats began to clap. She joined them, clapping so enthusiastically that her hands smarted. Under the blazing overhead lights, Irene looked lovelier than ever. She had appeared from somewhere behind the star-studded curtain.

"Hi, everybody!" she said brightly when the clapping had subsided. "Welcome to the Golden Girl show. In the half hour before we go on the air there's time to make you acquainted with some of the people important to the show."

One by one they were introduced. Irene knew all the technicians and called them by their first names —the manager with his walkie-talkie, the boom man, the camera men and their helpers. One was adjusting the seat on the dolly.

"I'd get dizzy up there," Judy whispered.

She had never before realized how many other people besides actors were needed to put on a TV show. The sound man, the lighting engineer, the director and his assistants in the control room—each had his own part to play.

"You people out there are part of the show, too," Irene continued. "When the hands of the studio clock point to seven we will go on the air. In the meantime, I'd like to present four of my best friends to the studio audience."

"She means us. How sweet of her!" exclaimed Judy.

"Me, too?" asked Clarissa, holding back a little as the others left their seats. "She can't mean me. I only met her today."

Judy laughed. "It doesn't take Irene long to decide who her friends are. Come on!"

CHAPTER VII

A Hidden Danger

THE area between the first row of seats and the Golden Girl set was filled with a complicated maze of technical equipment. Judy nearly tripped over a trailing cable on the way to join Irene on the studio floor.

"Come on," Judy urged Clarissa a second time.

Irene was waiting for them. She seemed completely at home on the studio floor, moving through and around the pieces of equipment as easily as she moved about in her kitchen at home. The girls were introduced. It was all very informal and nice. Afterwards the floor manager suggested a quick tour behind the scenes.

"I know you want to show your friends around, Irene," he said with an understanding twinkle in his eyes. "You have ten minutes."

"Thank you, Si. I won't take more than that. This doesn't compare with Radio City, of course," Irene apologized, turning to Judy, "but perhaps I can show you something you haven't already seen."

"What about the dressing rooms?" Judy thought of Clarissa's request and explained that they hadn't seen them on their other tour. "It was interrupted," she began and then stopped as there was too much to tell in ten minutes.

"How did that happen?" Irene asked.

"We'll explain it later," Judy promised. "Is there time to see the dressing rooms?"

"They're small and crowded tonight, but I guess we can take a quick peek," Irene agreed. "This way, girls! Be careful and don't fall over anything."

The dusty, cluttered space behind the glittering curtain was a disappointment to Clarissa. Judy could tell by the look on her face. Backgrounds were folded one against the other. Props waited to be placed inside make-believe rooms that were nothing but painted canvas stretched on wooden racks. Beyond, a narrow corridor separated two rows of doors.

"Will we see Francine Dow?" Clarissa asked suddenly.

Pauline looked at Flo and said pointedly, "We had a little argument over the color of her hair."

"You can settle it when you see her," Irene told them as they entered the crowded dressing room. The girls who were to be good fairies on the program were fluttering about in their filmy dresses. Two of them were seated before a long dressing table putting on make-up that gave their faces a yellowish tinge. A third girl, made up to look like an old woman, was dipping a sponge into a bowl of green stuff and then applying it to her face.

"She must be the witch," Pauline whispered to Judy. "Doesn't she *scare* you?"

"Her hair is green, too," Flo observed with a giggle. "How about washing your hair with *green* hair wash, Clarissa? You said you'd do anything to get on TV. Would you play the part of an old witch?"

"I—I don't know," she faltered. "I'd hate to make myself any uglier than I am."

Obviously the witch could hear the whispered conversation behind her. Making her voice sound old and cackling, she said without turning her head, "So you think I'm ugly, my pretty? Wait until you see the curse I put on the child! I hope I don't scare any little kiddies who may be watching—"

"You scare me," Clarissa interrupted. "I can see your face in the mirror."

"It's bad luck to look into a mirror over anyone's shoulder," the witch warned her. "Why don't you go away?"

"I'm sorry." Clarissa, her eyes still fixed on the mirrored face of the witch, was backing out into the corridor toward a closed door.

"Is that another dressing room, Irene?" asked Flo. "We didn't see your guest star, Francine Dow."

"Would you know her?" asked Judy. "I'm afraid I wouldn't. She's appeared in so many different roles. I don't even know what color her hair is."

"I'm afraid I don't either," Irene confessed. "She wore a black wig in the *Mikado* and looked quite like a Japanese schoolgirl. She is late, but I'm sure she'll

be here in time to play the part of the Sleeping Beauty. She doesn't appear until the show is half over. Maybe she planned to be late so she would have the dressing room to herself. We had to rehearse without her this afternoon," Irene continued, a worried note creeping into her voice, "but she assured me, over the telephone, that she knows the part."

"The play would be ruined without Sleeping Beauty, wouldn't it?" Clarissa asked. "I hope I haven't brought bad luck."

"Of course you haven't. That's just a silly superstition," Irene declared. "Actually, it makes an actress nervous to have anyone look over her shoulder when she's applying make-up, so she's apt to tell you it brings bad luck."

"I see."

Judy wondered if she did. "You say this isn't a dressing room? What is behind this other door?" she asked curiously.

She could hear voices that made her even more curious. "It's forbidden!" someone was almost shouting. "This thing is still in the experimental stage. It may be as dangerous as an atom bomb!"

"I don't know what all the excitement is about. This is our film storage room," Irene explained, tapping on the door before she opened it. "Most of our programs are on film or on kinescope, and they're kept here. Mine is one of the few live shows that originate in this studio."

She was calm as she entered the small room that was still charged with emotion. Rows of shelves and pigeonholes lined the walls. Two men were glaring at each other across a high desk.

"You look like a couple of roosters ready for a fight," Irene told them amiably. "Can you forget your differences long enough to meet some friends of mine? This is Mr. Lenz, our projectionist."

"How do you do," the older man said in an agitated voice as he was introduced to the four girls.

Judy recognized the younger man as the one with the unruly lock of brown hair.

"You were on the tour with us!" she exclaimed in surprise.

"You *are* from our agency! Why did you tell the guide you were from Hollywood?" Flo demanded.

"Usually," said the brown-haired young man with an easy smile, "I tell people what they want to hear. You want me to be Blake van Pelt, a native New Yorker. Yes, my dear Miss Garner, that is my name. I already know yours because, you see, I do work on Madison Avenue just as you do—and for the same agency, so I think we understand each other. The guide, another charming young lady, wanted me to be from out of town so I gave her a line."

"Did you say line or lie?" Flo was angry now and justifiably so, Judy thought. Without in the least understanding what was going on, she felt herself on the side of truth. Something Clarissa had said back in the restaurant flashed across her mind. "Doesn't anybody in New York care about the truth?" Apparently there were a number of people who did, among them the white-haired projectionist, Mr. Lenz.

"The word is lie," he said icily. "So you tell people what they want to hear, do you, Mr. van Pelt? I think the purpose of your agency is to make them dissatisfied with what they have so they'll buy what you have to sell."

The young man flashed another smile.

"You've put it very well. Advertising is a selling job. We're not in business to entertain people or to make them contented as they sit in their living rooms watching TV. Contented people are like cows. It's our job to make them discontented. That's no crime, is it, Mr. Lenz?"

"No, but this is! None of the other networks allow it. I have my orders from the director of this program," the projectionist declared. "Now, suppose you take your film out of here."

Young Blake van Pelt picked up a round gray can about an inch thick and a foot across, and sauntered out of the room. Did it contain a roll of film or something more sinister? Judy found herself wondering what Mr. Lenz meant when he had shouted, "It may be as dangerous as an atom bomb!" After he had calmed down a little the projectionist opened a can similar to the one the younger man had taken away with him and said to Irene, "This is the ad we'll run on your show, Mrs. Meredith. It's for a tooth paste approved by dentists, and features a cute little girl cleaning her teeth."

"It may inspire little Judy," Irene began and then stopped. "What was the other ad?" she asked. "Why were you so angry about it, Mr. Lenz?"

"An old man's temper," he replied. "Don't mind me, and good luck with your show tonight."

CHAPTER VIII

The Witch's Curse

"I'll need more than luck if anything is wrong in the film department," Irene said later when they were back on the studio floor.

She was worried about something. Judy could see that. She took the seat Pauline was saving for her. Flo was already seated next to Pauline with Clarissa occupying the chair next to the aisle. An usher was seating people in every available place.

"No empty seats! No empty seats!" he kept on repeating as the crowd surged in.

Two pedestal cameras were stationed directly in front of the curtain where Irene stood waiting. At one side, mounted on a large three-wheeled platform, rode the man who operated the mike boom. The man on the dolly was sitting in his funny little seat with the operator ready to raise or lower him.

The hands of the big studio clock over the exit

door moved slowly toward the hour of seven. The camera men and the boom man, all wearing headphones, stood ready before their equipment. The floor manager also waited for the directions he would receive through his headpiece.

"All set?" asked the announcer.

"All set," Irene replied, smiling.

Did Judy imagine it, or was her smile a little forced? "Nothing must go wrong," Judy caught herself almost praying. "Please, don't let anything go wrong."

"One minute . . . stand by!" sounded over the loudspeaker.

Were the other girls as tense as she was? Judy found it hard to read the expressions on their faces. The lights over the Golden Girl set made everything else look dim.

The television set suspended over the middle aisle was showing the end commercial from the previous show. As soon as it was over red lights flashed above the exit doors, and Judy knew Golden Girl was on the air. The announcer stepped to one side, out of camera range, and clapped his hands as a signal for the audience to clap.

"Isn't she lovely?" whispered someone in the audience as the bright spotlight shone down on Irene. Quick tears came to Judy's eyes as Irene began to sing:

"My own golden girl, there is one, only one,
Who has eyes like the stars and hair like the sun."

It was her theme song. Judy's thoughts took her back to the first time she had heard it on a roof garden while she danced with Dale Meredith.

"Irene is a golden girl tonight," he had said, and from then on her happiness had become his chief concern. Judy thought of him now, at home in their new Long Island house, probably holding a sleepy baby on his knee as he listened.

"That's Mommy," he would be saying to little Judy. Or perhaps there was no need to say it. By now Judy's little namesake must be well acquainted with the mysteries of TV.

"Better acquainted than I am," Judy thought ruefully.

She couldn't overcome the fear that something would go wrong with the show. Little Judy wouldn't see the microphone dangling over her mother's head. She wouldn't see the cameras being moved in like menacing monsters. She wouldn't know, as Judy did, that somewhere back in the film room there had been something "as dangerous as an atom bomb."

"If Peter were here I could ask him about it," Judy thought.

"The advertising is over, and the show is about to begin," Pauline whispered.

Judy glimpsed the little girl cleaning her teeth on the TV set. Since the advertising was all on film, it did not seem to interrupt the play that was now beginning.

"Look!" she heard Clarissa whisper. "It's the palace

scene with the king and queen. I wonder if that's a real baby in the crib."

On the television screen the king and queen seemed to be crooning over a real baby, but Judy suspected the crib was empty. The throne room was only a painted scene on a wooden frame with a few props in the foreground to make it appear real. The spotlight rested on the royal family for a moment and then moved over to Irene. Dressed as one of the fairies, she sang to summon the others:

> *"Fairies! Fairies! Now appear*
> *Bringing gifts for baby dear.*
> *One will give a pretty face,*
> *Two a body full of grace,*
> *Three the love light in her eyes.*
> *Four will make her kind and wise."*

In danced the fairies bringing their gifts and waving their wands over the crib. On the screen flecks of stardust could be seen swirling about. Remembering the tour, Judy knew how this effect was achieved.

More gifts were bestowed on the little princess as the next seven fairies danced in. Irene's song was as beautiful and tender as a lullaby. A film strip of a real baby made it seem as if the audience had been given a glimpse of the little princess in her crib.

It was almost too real when the witch whirled in. A gasp went up from the audience as she interrupted the fairy song with a hoarse shriek:

> *"I was not invited. Why?*
> *For punishment I'll make her* die!"

"No, oh, no!" Judy almost forgot it was a play and found herself crying out with the fairies. All had given their gifts except Irene, who was playing the part of the twelfth fairy.

The queen, rising from her throne, began to explain that there were only twelve golden plates for feasting.

"That is why you weren't invited, dear, good fairy," she said to the witch. "Please take away your curse."

> *"For shame!" cried the witch. "I'll make it worse*
> *She shall live to age fifteen,*
> *But she shall never be a queen.*
> *While spinning she shall prick her hand.*
> *There'll be no cure in all the land."*

"Have pity! Have pity!" cried the poor queen, wringing her hands and sobbing so realistically that Judy almost cried with her.

"I will have every spinning wheel destroyed," the king declared. "This cruel pronouncement must not come to pass."

"Can't you help us, dear fairies?" sobbed the queen.

They drooped like wilted flowers. "I'm afraid not," one after another of them replied. "She is not one of us. She is a witch. Her powers are greater than ours, but we will try."

At that they began dancing around the witch, trying to touch her with their wands. The music played wildly as the witch whirled and danced, always eluding them and finally dancing off the set.

"She's gone!" exclaimed the king. "She's left her curse on all of us."

"You good fairies, is there nothing you can do?" The queen turned to the dancers with a pleading gesture. Eleven of them shook their heads. Irene, the twelfth fairy, danced into the spotlight and began to sing:

"*A twelfth gift I have yet to give.*
The princess shall not die, but live.
A fairy mist will change the spell
From death to sleep. She shall sleep well
A hundred years. Yes, all shall sleep.
Change, curse, from death to slumber deep!"

With a wave of her wand, Irene stepped out of camera range and stood smiling and bowing to the studio audience as the curtain descended. Judy forgot to look at the advertising. She was seeing only Irene.

"She's the star of this show. Francine Dow can't be any more wonderful than she was," Judy whispered.

"I hope she's here."

Was Pauline worried, too? Clarissa was heard to whisper, "Oh dear, I left my two bottles of shampoo back there in the witch's dressing room."

"You can get them after the show," Flo whispered back. She turned to Pauline and said something about the commercial. Several people left their seats during the intermission, but Judy stayed where she was. She didn't want to miss anything.

As soon as the commercial was over, the cameras

were again on Irene. She stood in front of the curtain.

"The king has issued a decree commanding that every spindle in the kingdom be burnt, but it is no use," she said sadly. "Fifteen years have passed. The witch's curse is almost forgotten, but look what's hidden away in a dusty old room at the top of the castle!"

The curtain opened on the set she had described. There, before an old spinning wheel, sat the witch spinning flax. For a time nothing was heard except the whir of the spinning wheel. Then a door opened, and a lovely young girl tiptoed in. Judy breathed a sigh of relief.

"It's Francine Dow! Her hair is golden just as I knew it was," Pauline whispered.

"It could be a wig," Flo whispered back.

The princess stood behind the old witch, not saying a word until she turned her head. Then, appearing frightened, she said, "Good day, my good lady, what are you doing here?"

"I am spinning," said the witch, nodding her head.

"What thing is that which twists round so merrily?"

"It is a spindle. Want to try it, my pretty?"

It was the same evil voice Judy had heard back in the dressing room.

"I—I'm afraid."

The princess did sound afraid as she took the spindle. Her long golden hair fell almost to her waist. Were those real tears in her eyes when she pricked her finger? She fell, almost immediately, in an undramatic pose with her face turned away from the audience. The witch, chuckling softly to herself, began to chant:

> *"My curse is done. The sleep of death*
> *Shall take away the princess' breath!"*

Judy drew a breath of her own that was almost a gasp. She knew the old fairy story by heart, and yet there was a moment when the play seemed so real that she wasn't at all sure the curse wouldn't come true.

CHAPTER IX

Into the Mist

"Isn't it spooky?" Pauline whispered, breaking the spell that was upon Judy. The theater was so dark she couldn't see her friend, but she could hear her voice. She was about to answer when the sound of a wailing siren reached her ears.

"What's *that?*" she questioned fearfully.

Pauline touched her arm. "Judy! You're all goose-flesh," she whispered. "It's only an ambulance. Probably there was an accident outside. But don't worry about it. We're safe enough in here."

"I hope we are." Judy had thought, for just a fleeting moment, that something might have happened back in the film room. Maybe an explosion or a fire. But common sense told her Pauline was right. Her attention was drawn back to the set where the fairies were now singing:

59

"The witch! The witch! Her curse came true.
Pray tell us, what can fairies do?"

"Nothing, my pretties!" chuckled the witch. She nodded her head so that the green hair fell in straggly wisps across her ugly face and repeated, "Nothing, my pretties. You can do nothing at all."

"Not so! Not so!" cried all the fairies, rushing at her in a wild dance, their feet flying faster and faster as the music increased in tempo.

Judy and her friends sat in rapt attention as did the entire audience. The siren outside could still be heard wailing above the music, but nobody paid much attention to it. Irene, leading her train of fairies, drove the witch into the wings and returned to where the princess had fallen.

"She only sleeps. She is not dead.
We'll take her to her royal bed,"

the fairies sang softly. Making cradles of their arms, they lifted the sleeping princess and carried her to another set where she was placed in a canopied bed to sleep for a hundred years.

"Isn't she beautiful?" Judy whispered. "She looks—"

"Watch!" Pauline interrupted as the cameras turned quickly on another set showing the kitchen of the castle. Here the cook fell asleep just as she was raising her hand to box the ears of the kitchen boy. In still another room the king and queen fell asleep on their thrones. Finally the audience was given a glimpse of the castle itself. It was only a background painting pulled down to hide the various sets, but it looked real enough on the television screen. Irene, standing in front of it, waved her wand and began to chant:

> *"Arise, oh misty vapors, rise*
> *To hide from all beneath the skies*
> *The place where Sleeping Beauty lies."*

"Look!" whispered Judy. "Now I know why everything is so misty. Steam is being blown from a big black kettle over there to the right."

The mist was now very dense. A fan was blowing it across the set. When it cleared away the castle had changed. A thick growth of weeds and brush made it seem as if a hundred years had passed during the brief pause for the commercial.

All this time Irene had been standing to the left of the set. She introduced the prince, now seen in a puzzled pose before the forsaken castle.

"What's this?" he cried. "A lovely castle now appears. The mist has hidden it for years."

Parting the thorny bushes, he made his way toward it. Suddenly, to Judy's surprise, the whole background scene went up like a window shade, revealing the rooms inside the castle.

"There's Sleeping Beauty again! Isn't she lovely?" a voice behind Judy whispered.

"And so young looking!" another whispered. "Isn't it wonderful that Francine Dow can still play the part of a fifteen-year-old girl?"

The face of the actress was turned a little away from the viewers. A veil covered it. She lay as still as death until the prince lifted the veil and kissed her. Then quickly, almost too quickly, it seemed to Judy, the play ended and Irene was before the cameras singing her closing song. She sang it all the way through. When it was finished, she blew a kiss to the children in the audience, adding, "And here's one for you, Judykins." Little Judy was always Judykins to her adoring young mother.

"Francine Dow wasn't really the star. Irene was," declared Judy as the red lights flashed off. Almost immediately the prop men began dismantling the set. Fairyland backgrounds disappeared. Cameras were pushed aside. The magic spell that had held the audience was over.

"Where's Clarissa?" Pauline Faulkner asked suddenly.

Judy looked around for the girl they had met in the restaurant, but she was nowhere in sight. The seat next to Flo was vacant. Judy tried to think when she had last seen Clarissa or heard her speak. A shivery feeling came over her.

"Didn't you see her leave?" Pauline was asking Florence Garner.

Flo shook her head. "I wasn't looking at anything except the play," she replied. "Wasn't it beautiful when that fairy mist covered the castle and made it vanish?"

Judy waved her hand in front of Flo's eyes. "The play's over. Come back from fairyland," she told her.

"Clarissa has vanished. You were sitting right beside her. You must have seen her when she left her seat."

"She didn't leave it. Anyway, not that I noticed," Flo protested. "Maybe she was a phantom after all. Maybe she disappeared into the mist."

"If she did, she disappeared with the money we lent her," Pauline declared.

"Good heavens!" This statement brought Flo out of her trancelike state. She stared at the empty seat and then at Pauline. "Well, what do you know?" she said at last. "I think all four of us, including Irene, have been played for suckers. We should have known better than to trust a stranger. We don't even know where she lives."

"I thought she was a phony. What do you think, Judy?" asked Pauline.

"I still can't believe it," Judy declared. "Clarissa was our friend."

"Our phantom friend," Pauline reminded her.

"It is sort of weird, isn't it?" agreed Judy. "We called her a phantom and then she—well, she just vanished. I can't think how or where. Was she there when we heard that siren, Flo?"

"What siren?"

Apparently Flo had been so engrossed in the show that she hadn't heard it.

"It was an ambulance we heard outside the theater right after the witch put her curse on Sleeping Beauty. An ambulance!" Judy exclaimed, a new possibility dawning upon her. "Do you suppose Clarissa—"

"Of course not," Pauline interrupted. "She was in

"Who was in that ambulance?" Judy inquired

here watching the show, not outside on the street."

"We don't know that," Judy objected. "We don't know how long her seat has been vacant. She could have slipped outside, for some reason, and been hurt in an accident. Come on, girls! We have to find out for sure."

Grabbing their coats, they hurried outside to see what had happened. They were just too late. The ambulance with its wailing siren had already disappeared down the street. At the curb a taxicab with its rear fender smashed in was waiting to be towed away. The crowd that had gathered around the scene of the accident was beginning to thin. Judy spied a policeman and rushed over to him.

"We can't find our friend. We think she may have left the theater and been hurt or something. Who was in that ambulance?" she inquired all in one breath.

CHAPTER X

The Wrong Direction

Judy knew a moment of panic. When she tried to describe Clarissa all she could remember was her hair. She called it honey colored while Pauline and Flo described it as dark blond.

"She was pretty," they all agreed. "She looked a little like—well, like Francine Dow. She's the guest star who played Sleeping Beauty," Judy added.

"She wasn't that pretty," Flo objected quickly. "Her hair was dull, and she had a rather drab look about her. She was young—"

"How young?" the policeman asked.

"About sixteen."

"The woman they took away in the ambulance can't be your missing friend if that's the way it is," the policeman said reassuringly. "No one could call her sixteen. Besides, she was hurt on her way to the theater—not coming away from it. The taxi driver says she kept after him to hurry. He turned the corner too fast and skidded into another car. Fortunately, no one in the second vehicle was hurt. But here's the cab driver," he ended abruptly. "He can tell you about it himself."

Judy was introduced to the cab driver, who was a little shaken up, but not hurt. More than anything else, he seemed concerned about his passenger.

"Friend of yours?" he inquired.

Judy didn't know what to say. Was Clarissa a friend or wasn't she? Had she deceived them as Pauline and Flo seemed to think? It was Pauline who described the missing girl and took down the name of the hospital where the victim of the accident was taken.

"She couldn't have been Clarissa. She was going in the wrong direction," Flo told Pauline.

"Where did she hail your cab?" Judy asked finally.

"Grand Central Station," he replied. "She said she'd just arrived in town and had to get to the theater in a hurry. She didn't say why. Just gave me the address and a big tip and told me to step on it as she was already late—"

"She certainly was if she expected to see the Sleeping Beauty show. She'd already missed the best part of it."

"Do you mean the witch dance?" the cab driver asked. "She said something about that."

"What else did she say?" Judy asked eagerly.

"Don't know. I don't listen much," the cab driver

confessed. "I got my own problems. If this dame don't come to—"

"Was she badly hurt?" Pauline interrupted.

"Out like a light. Couldn't give her name or anything. I wish you girls did know her. It would be a help. She was what I'd call the theatrical type," the cab driver continued. "Older than you, but sort of young looking—if you get what I mean."

"What color was your passenger's hair?" asked Judy.

The cab driver's answer startled her. "Red," he replied. "But not natural looking like yours. Think you know her?"

"I'm sure we don't. It's funny she mentioned the witch dance, though," Flo said thoughtfully as the three girls turned away. "If there's any truth in that story Clarissa told us—"

Pauline broke in with a laugh.

"You aren't entertaining the idea that she might really be a changeling, are you?"

"No, but it did frighten her when that witch whirled in."

"You remember that? You know she was sitting beside you then?" Pauline questioned.

"I remember it, too," put in Judy. "I heard her say she'd left her two bottles of shampoo back there on the witch's dressing table. Maybe she went backstage after them."

"If she went anywhere," Pauline said grimly, "it was for the reason I mentioned. She had our twenty dollars, didn't she?"

"She said her father is a minister. I'll bet he is—not!" scoffed Flo. "And Irene was telling me she didn't think some advertising was honest! I wonder what she'll say when she hears that our phantom friend disappeared with the money we lent her."

"But Flo, maybe she didn't," Judy protested. "Maybe she's back there in the theater looking for us."

"That could be exactly where she is," agreed Pauline. "Let's ask Irene if she knows what happened to her. I'm sure our phantom friend didn't disappear into the mist."

Judy shivered at the way she said it. Remembering the film storage room and the secret it held, anything seemed possible. A real chill went through her as they reentered the theater. The overhead lights had been turned off, and the seats were all empty. The cameras, idle now, looked more like monsters than ever in the semidarkness. Most of the technicians had gone home, but there was some activity backstage where props were being put away. Voices came from the dressing room. Irene was saying, "I wonder where they went."

"We went outside if it's us you're wondering about," replied Judy, popping in at the door. Her entrance was so sudden that Irene jumped. The witch, who was just removing her green make-up, dropped her artificial nose. Pauline and Flo laughed, but their faces sobered when they attempted to describe the accident and their fears for Clarissa.

"We thought at first she might have taken a cab,

but the cab was coming from Grand Central terminal and it had a redheaded woman in it. She was taken to the hospital—"

"You're sure it wasn't Clarissa?" Irene interrupted.

"We're not sure of anything," Flo replied with a shiver. "Clarissa is a strange girl. One minute she was there beside me, and the next time I looked she was gone. She probably sneaked out with the money we lent her. I was under the spell of the play and didn't see her leave."

"You see how good you were," Irene said to the girl who had played the part of the witch. With her make-up removed, Judy could see that she was quite an ordinary-looking person. Her cackling voice, too, had been an act.

"Most people enjoy being frightened," the girl said. "But I hope I didn't upset your friend."

Clarissa was not in the dressing room. Neither were the two bottles of shampoo she claimed she had left there.

"She must have taken them. Did you see her come back here?" Judy asked.

Irene shook her head. "I thought she was out there with you watching the play. I looked for you afterwards. I wanted to introduce you to Francine Dow, but her aunt hurried her away as soon as we went off the air. I'm not sure, but I don't think she was quite well. Maybe she had a sore throat or something. She didn't sing to the prince—"

"Was she supposed to?" Pauline interrupted to ask.

"Yes, at the end. I sang my whole theme song to fill in. Was it very noticeable?"

"It was beautiful, Irene. *You* were the star," Judy declared warmly. "Francine Dow played her part well, of course, but I liked best the part where you danced around the baby."

"Did it look like a real baby in the crib? It wasn't," Irene explained. "It was only one of little Judy's dolls. She knew we were going to use it. I told her we'd make it look like a real baby, but she didn't understand about the film strip."

"Will she think her doll came to life?"

"Perhaps. When she's older I'll explain it. To her television is a magic box where just about anything can happen."

Judy thought about this a minute. The thought troubled her. Anything? She had a feeling something had happened—something she didn't like at all. The film storage room was searched but yielded no clue to the disappearance of Clarissa.

"There's nothing dangerous here, is there?" asked Judy, remembering the argument between the projectionist and the man from Flo's agency.

Irene opened one of the waffle-shaped cans to show her the roll of film inside.

"This is a spot commercial for the golden hair wash people," she said. "You couldn't call that dangerous, even though young girls who use it would look so much lovelier with their own natural shade of hair."

"I didn't mean that. I'm not sure just what I did mean."

The can of film looked innocent enough, but the fear that had gripped Judy stayed with her. Mr. Lenz had been justifiably angry, and the danger, whatever it was, had been real.

CHAPTER XI

On the Train

"I guess we'll just have to go home and forget Clarissa," Pauline said finally after they had searched the whole theater and questioned everybody—technicians as well as actors who were still there in the cast. Some had already left, but those who remained could tell them nothing.

"She fainted before," Judy remembered.

Irene heard, for the first time, how Clarissa had looked into a mirror and seen no reflection. "And then," Flo went on telling her, "something went wrong with that closed circuit TV set where we were supposed to see our pictures, and she didn't show. That was when she fainted. We took her to the first aid room and then went back and finished our tour. The TV set was all right. All the rest of us showed. We forgot to ask the guide if she knew what went wrong with it. Clarissa wouldn't go back there. She was afraid."

"Of what?" asked Irene.

"That she wasn't real, I guess. I'm beginning to be afraid of it myself," Flo admitted. "The doorman said nobody left the show early, and nobody left by the stage entrance except a few people who were in the cast."

"Francine Dow was one of them, wasn't she? What about her aunt?" asked Judy. "You said she left with her."

"That's right. I forgot about her," Irene admitted. "She left by the stage entrance, too. I know what you're thinking, Judy, but she was an old lady. Well, anyway, middle-aged. She was a plump, motherly looking woman with gray hair. I noticed her earlier in the studio audience."

"When Clarissa was still there?"

"Yes, it was before the show went on the air. I guess Francine had planned to meet her aunt afterwards and go home with her. They probably left in a hurry because Francine wasn't feeling well and wanted to avoid meeting people. I heard her aunt say something about a week end in the country. We could find out where they went and question them, I suppose, but I'm sure it wouldn't do any good."

"It might," Judy said hopefully. "They might have seen Clarissa."

"I doubt it," Pauline replied. "If she deliberately ran off with the money we lent her, she would have made sure she wasn't seen. Obviously, that's what happened."

It did seem obvious.

"We never should have trusted her in the first place," Pauline went on. "That story she told must have been part of her plan to trick us and make us sorry for her. It isn't possible for a girl to look in a mirror and see no reflection. Things like that only happen in ghost stories."

"This is a ghost story," Flo said in an awed tone, "only it's happening to us. Maybe she wasn't real. She didn't show—"

Pauline turned to her friend. "Flo, you aren't going to believe—?" she began.

But Irene cut in, "In phantoms? Of course she isn't. What's your theory, Judy? You always come up with something."

"I will," Judy promised. "Just give me time. It would help if we knew exactly when she disappeared."

"Wasn't it just about the time that misty haze covered the set?" Flo questioned. "What was it, anyway, some new kind of vapor to make people vanish?" she asked nervously.

"It was only steam," Irene reassured her. "I couldn't see what was going on backstage from where I was standing, but I had a good view of that steam kettle. There was nothing unnatural about it."

"No?" Flo sounded dubious. "Maybe not, but there was something strange about Clarissa. Vanishing like that—it's utterly fantastic!"

"I have a few fantastic theories of my own," Judy

admitted. "If she'd had time to use that golden hair wash—"

"What do you think's in it? Vanishing cream?" Pauline was laughing. Her theory was really the only sensible one, Judy decided. She was eager to talk it over with Peter. He knew so much more about the workings of the criminal mind than she did. There were patterns of behavior. Would Clarissa's behavior fit one of them? Somehow Judy doubted it.

"I suppose we shouldn't have trusted her," she said at last. "Her innocent appearance didn't fool the cashier in the restaurant. But I'm not sorry if it fooled us. Peter might not agree with me, but I believe in trusting people. Clarissa may be involved in some sort of confidence game. And yet, somehow, I believe she is a friend. I mean a real one."

"You're a real friend to her, Judy." Irene shook her head. "It's beyond me. I suppose she'll go home, wherever her home is, and we'll never see her again. It was an experience, anyway."

Judy found she couldn't dismiss it that lightly. Too many experiences had crowded in to make her vacation in New York not at all what she had anticipated. First there had been her discovery that Tower House was no longer standing. It appeared to have vanished but, in reality, it had only been torn down to make room for a new apartment building. Irene and Dale were now living in a more modern house farther out on Long Island.

Weird things had happened in Tower House as they had in Judy's own home both before and after her

marriage to Peter Dobbs. She would never forget the
time she saw the transparent figure floating about in
her garden. Blackberry, her cat, had provided the clue
to that mystery as well as to the latest one she and
Peter had solved. Always there had been a solution.
The only real ghosts, Judy had discovered, were such
things as suspicion and fear. Some fear could be haunt-
ing Clarissa.

"She must be somewhere," Judy said as they left
the theater. They took a taxi, not without misgivings.

"Don't ask the driver to hurry," Flo warned them.
"The streets are still slippery. Remember what happened to the woman with the red hair."

"Like mine," Judy recalled thoughtfully, "only not
as natural looking. We don't know what happened to
her. I'd like to meet her and ask her a few questions.
I wonder if she has regained consciousness."

"I'll call the hospital tomorrow and find out," Pauline promised. "Drop me off first, please," she told
the driver. "Then the others want to drive on to
Penn Station."

"That's where we take the Long Island Railroad,"
Irene explained. "Flo goes home by train, too, but
on a different line."

Judy found the railroad station confusing. People
were hurrying this way and that. There was an upper
level and a lower level and ever so many turns before
they reached a crowded section of the station where
Flo bade them good-by and left them to join another
line of people. It seemed to Judy that half the city
must be commuting to Long Island by train.

"I like to watch all the different faces, don't you?" she whispered to Irene. "Clarissa could be in this crowd—"

Presently a man in uniform opened a gate, and the crowd surged through. Judy and Irene found seats on the train, but not together. A man, concealed by his open newspaper, occupied the place next to the window. All the seats were soon filled, and the train started on its way. Irene, who was sitting just behind Judy, tapped her shoulder.

"We can't talk much. The train is making too much noise," she said above the creaks and rattles.

"That's all right. I'm a little tired, anyway," Judy confessed. "It's been a long day."

"Why don't you lean back and close your eyes?" Irene suggested. "I will, too. It's an hour's ride—" A yawn came, interrupting the sentence.

"I won't sleep," Judy told herself when she saw that Irene was resting. "I'll have to keep my eyes open to watch for our station."

The conductor, she discovered a little later, was calling the stations. She roused herself to listen, dozing between stops. But it was only her conscious mind that slept. The thoughts she could control were at rest, but other thoughts came unbidden. *My hair is dull. My hair is drab.* But those were Clarissa's thoughts! They rushed on with the train. *Dull! Drab! Dull! Drab!*—faster and faster.

As the unwanted thoughts pounded in Judy's head the train swayed, first this way and then that way. A frail old lady making her way down the aisle changed suddenly to a young girl with golden hair. Judy stared at her. Then she looked at the girl sitting beside her and saw that she, too, had golden hair. Her face was blank like the face of a department-store dummy. *It was a man before! He had been reading a newspaper!* How had the strange transformation taken place? Had it happened this way to Clarissa?

Behind Judy sat another girl with a blank face and golden hair. Another one was in front and still another across the aisle. The train, moving backwards now, seemed full of golden-haired girls with identical faces. Judy's thoughts, too, were moving in a reverse direction. Now she was at the station backing through the gates. All the golden-haired people surged forward, pressing closer and closer until she could scarcely breathe. She tried to call to them in protest. At last, as if from a great distance, she heard her own voice whispering Irene's name. She tried desperately to speak louder and presently the cry came.

"Irene!"

With that she swayed and would have fallen sideways if the man with the newspaper hadn't caught her. Irene was at her side. Unaccountably, they were back in the train.

"How—where—what?" Judy stammered. She was awake now, but the feeling that a crowd of golden-haired people were suffocating her still lingered.

"What happened? Where are we?" she managed to ask.

CHAPTER XII

A Night of Terror

Irene's reply was hurried. "We're *here*. Come on, Judy! Wake up!"

"I am awake. What happened to all the golden-haired people? They were suffocating me. They—"

"Come *on!*" Irene interrupted, pulling Judy to her feet just as the train lurched to a stop. People began to get off. Judy saw now that they were all kinds of people—men, women, even a drowsy child on one man's shoulder. The hair that showed below their hats was black, brown, straight and curly. Their faces were no longer blank. Each had its own individuality. Dark faces, fair faces—how beautiful they suddenly were, and how different!

"I dreamed," Judy managed to say, "that they were all alike. It was a terrible, a frightening dream.

I never have nightmares, especially on trains. What happened?"

"Nothing," Irene replied, laughing, "but something will if we don't hurry. The train will take us past our station. I was asleep, too. We nearly missed it. Wait!" she called to the conductor.

"You getting off here?" he inquired. "Hurry up. I'll hold the train."

It started again with a jolt almost as soon as Judy and Irene stepped down to the platform.

"That was close. People have been killed getting off moving trains," Irene said with a shudder.

Bewildered, Judy looked around her. "Isn't anybody going to meet us?" she inquired.

"Dale didn't know which train we were going to take. We'll go home by taxi," Irene announced.

She hailed a cab that was just about to pull away from the station. She and Judy were crowded in along with other passengers who lived in the same suburban town. Again Judy had that elated sense of being glad —glad that they were different.

"How terrible it would be if we were all alike," she said to Irene as they huddled together in the crowded taxi. "Our faces, our hair, our thoughts— everything. Would you like it if everyone in the whole world had golden hair and a face like yours?"

"I'd hate it," Irene replied. "It's bad enough when I buy a dress and find out someone else has one like it. Why do you ask such a question?"

"It was that way in my dream. I told you—"

"I wasn't listening. You'll have to tell me again

when we're home. After all, it was only a dream."

"Was it?"

"What do you think it was?" Irene inquired.

"A prophecy, maybe. People used to have prophetic visions. Maybe, some time in the future—"

The cab stopped to let two of the passengers out. Irene lived in a beautiful neighborhood. The houses, like the people who lived in them, were all different. Behind them were tall trees, outlined against the night sky, and a brook that reminded Judy of Dry Brook at home. An innocent brook and yet, when it had poured its flood waters into the pond above the Roulsville dam . . . Judy shuddered at the memory.

"Horace dreamed the dam would break—and it did!" she said suddenly. "I can still hear the roar and feel the horror—before I knew the people would be saved. Irene, there could be another flood—"

"What flood?"

"A flood of advertising. Don't laugh. Flo asked me to talk you into accepting that offer—"

"There's no need," Irene broke in. "I've already decided. Flo's right. It's silly of me to feel the way I do about commercials. If I can get a sponsor there's no reason why I shouldn't be on the big network. Dale thinks I should. There he is at the window motioning for us to hurry," Irene observed as the cab stopped to let them out. "Oh, I do hope little Judy is all right. There's a light in her room."

There were lights all over the house. Dale's anxious face told Judy that something was wrong. He started to say something to her, but Irene broke in.

"It's little Judy. I know it."

Saying this, she hurried into the baby's room with Judy close behind her. Little Judy was awake. Apparently she had reached over and turned on the light by herself.

"I heard Daddy on the tefelone," she announced solemnly. Then, with a little jump, she landed in Irene's arms and began to hug her. Judy could see that she was perfectly all right. But something was wrong. She could feel it.

"You comed out of the TV. I saw you, Mommy," the baby continued her chatter. "I saw the bad witch, too. She *skeered* me!"

"Did she, lamb? I'm so sorry."

"Oh, that's all right, Mommy. I like to be skeered."

"Were you thinking about the witch? Is that why you couldn't go to sleep?" asked Judy.

"I did sleep. Daddy woke me up. He was talking on the tefelone."

"Don't you love the way she says *telephone?*" Irene exclaimed, hugging little Judy again. "I was so sure something had happened to her, but if it was just the telephone—"

"Maybe Peter called up. We didn't give Dale a chance to tell us—"

Dale, in the doorway, interrupted Judy.

"It was the hospital. I tried to call you, but you had already left the theater. We can be thankful it isn't any worse—"

"What isn't?" asked Judy. "Why did the hospital call? What hospital was it?"

Dale mentioned the name of the hospital.

"Judy, isn't that where you said they took that red-headed woman?" Irene questioned.

"Yes, but they wouldn't call Dale about her. She's a stranger. If someone we know was hurt. If Peter—"

"It *is* Peter. I tried to break the news gently," Dale said in so grave a tone that Judy found herself staring at him in silent terror.

"Dale, what has happened?" she cried when she could find her voice. "Why is he in the hospital? What are they going to do to him?"

"They're going to operate—"

"But why? Why? Peter is never sick. He must be hurt. Was he—was he—" The word wouldn't come. Judy knew Peter's work was dangerous. She knew, too, that his latest assignment was one of his biggest. He couldn't discuss it, but he had said, just before he left, "Wish me luck, Angel. This is something really big."

To an FBI man, something big was usually a raid. Peter carried a gun but seldom used it. "Criminals carry guns, too," thought Judy. Aloud she said, "Tell me the truth, Dale. Was Peter—shot?"

Dale nodded, adding quickly, "It could have been worse. They're going to operate to remove a bullet from his shoulder. There's not much danger—"

"But there is a little. He came close to being killed, didn't he? How soon can I see him?" Judy questioned breathlessly.

"The hospital will call—"

"When? When?"

"When the operation is over. Meantime, why don't you try and get a little rest? You can stretch out here on the sofa, Judy, until the telephone rings," Dale suggested.

Judy shook her head. "I couldn't sleep. I'm going back to New York—I want to be at the hospital—"

"In the middle of the night?" Irene shook her head. "You'll do Peter more good if you're not exhausted when you see him."

This silenced Judy. She knew it would be better to try and get some rest as Dale suggested. "I won't sleep," she told herself when Dale and Irene had left her alone in the dimly lighted living room. She remembered thinking the same thing just before she fell asleep on the train. The sofa was long and low—like a train. Again she could hear the clanking wheels as they rumbled out the words, "Dull, drab, dull, drab . . ." faster and faster. Once more she was crowded in, almost suffocated by the throng of golden-haired people. She was looking for Peter. But she could see nothing but blank faces topped by golden curls.

"Peter, where are you?" came the voiceless cry.

Judy awoke from her dream of terror to hear the telephone ringing. She sprang toward it, half asleep, jerked the instrument from its resting place, and asked breathlessly, "Is this the hospital? How is he?"

"It's Honey." The voice of Peter's sister seemed to come from very far away. "They called us, since they couldn't reach you. How is he, Judy? And how are

"Is this the hospital?" she asked breathlessly

you taking it? I couldn't sleep. I just had to call and find out how everything is."

"Everything's terrible," wailed Judy. "I don't know how Peter is. I couldn't find him in the parade of golden-haired, faceless people. Honey, promise me!"

"I'll promise anything," came the sympathetic voice over the wire.

"Then promise—" Judy paused, trying to shake off the web of sleep that seemed to be holding her prisoner. Then, to her own surprise and Honey's horror, she finished, "Promise me you won't do anything to change the color of your hair!"

CHAPTER XIII

Before Daylight

"JUDY, are you well?" Honey's voice held a note of deep anxiety. She was calling all the way from Farringdon, Judy knew. Judy hadn't meant to worry her. But how could she explain what she had just said when she didn't understand it herself?

"I mean—" Now Honey was floundering for the right words. "Was it too much of a shock—about Peter? Or were you just trying to change the subject? This is certainly a strange time to be asking me about my hair."

"I know. I was half asleep. Forgive me," Judy said. "I was dreaming, I guess. This is the second time I've had the same dream. It still seems horribly real. I am worried, of course. I'm still waiting for the hospital to call."

"Then I'll hang up so they can."

"Wait a minute. Talk a little more," Judy begged finally. "I need the reassurance of your voice."

"That's more like the Judy I know. Don't worry. Peter will be all right, and then you'll stop dreaming."

"But I had the dream before I knew he was hurt," Judy protested.

"Don't ask me to explain it. I'm no good at that sort of thing. Remember that old dream book, Judy? I'll hunt it up, if you want me to, and find out what it means to dream of faceless people—"

"With golden hair." Judy stopped herself quickly and said, "Don't bother, Honey. The dream doesn't matter any more. It's Peter—"

"I know, dear. Call me back when you have news."

Judy promised that she would. She felt better after talking with Honey. Now she was wide awake. Irene, hearing her up, tiptoed out into the living room.

"Any news?" she asked.

"Not yet," replied Judy. "That was Honey on the phone. It seems ages ago that we were pretending she was at the table with us. So much has happened since then—Clarissa's disappearance, and now Peter. I want to go to him, Irene. I'm not tired any more. I can sit in the hospital waiting room and be there when he wakes up. The Long Island trains run all night, don't they?"

Irene consulted a timetable that was tacked to a bulletin board beside the telephone. "We just missed the two fifty-eight. This is Sunday morning. The trains don't run very often. There isn't another one until five o'clock. But we can drive in if you want to. We can bundle little Judy into the back seat, and she'll never know the difference. Want to?"

"Yes, I do want to," Judy replied gratefully. "I can't stand this waiting."

"You poor dear!" Irene sympathized. "We hoped you would get a little more sleep. Dale!" she called to her husband. "Judy wants us to drive in."

"I rather thought she would."

He appeared all dressed and ready. Irene had not undressed. Little Judy was carried to the car, blankets and all. She stirred once, said, "Go way, witch!" in a sleepy voice and then cuddled down to sleep again.

"That witch did scare her," Irene began in a worried tone.

"Of course she did. She was meant to," Dale broke in with a reassuring grin. "I wish you could have seen little Judy's eyes when you came in with your magic wand to chase the witch away. It was symbolic of hope chasing away fear, and beautifully done, my dear. I was very proud of you. Sleeping Beauty herself was something of a disappointment."

"She was?"

"Oh, I don't mean she wasn't beautiful and all that. Francine Dow is a girl of many faces. She did manage to look young and frightened if that was the effect she was trying to achieve. You could hardly see her face for that golden wig."

"Was it a wig?" asked Judy. "I thought it was the

natural color of her hair. I'm afraid I still don't know whether it's black, brown or golden."

Irene laughed. "Very few actresses can keep the natural color of their hair. They're the real change-lings. They change their hair and even their faces to suit the various parts they have to play."

"It may be all right for actresses, but for the rest of us—"

"Don't worry about it," Irene advised. "I know that dream upset you, but can't you see that it wasn't real? It couldn't happen that way."

"If everybody listened to the advertising on TV there'd be a lot more golden-haired people than there are now. There'd be too many. You'd see yourself coming and going just like the parade of golden-haired people in my dream. Everybody whose hair wasn't golden would be thinking, 'Your hair is dull. Your hair is drab!'—just the way I did."

"Why?" asked Dale, looking past Irene's golden head to Judy's mop of curly red hair. "How anyone could say a thing like that about either of you is more than I can understand."

"I can't understand it either," Judy admitted, "but it's true. I kept hearing *dull*, *drab*, until even the train wheels seemed to be repeating it. If I didn't have red hair and if I hadn't been teased all my life about how bright it is—"

"Well, what would you do?" asked Irene when Judy hesitated.

"I'd wash my hair with that golden hair wash. I did

buy some for you," Judy confessed when Irene made no comment. Dale was busy with his driving, and Judy sat between them in the front seat of the car. There was hardly any traffic this early in the morning, but there was a heavy fog that made it hard for Dale to see more than a few feet ahead.

"For me?" Irene asked incredulously. "Why on earth would you buy that stuff for me?"

"I don't know," Judy confessed. "I don't like the way I've been thinking things without knowing why I thought them. Peter never lets anything turn him from his convictions. I had a feeling, on the train, that something was wrong, while I was dreaming. I couldn't know about Peter. But I did know something was wrong."

Judy had been trying to hide her worry, but it was no use. They talked of many things as the car sped on toward the hospital. But their thoughts were with Peter. New York's skyline could be seen but faintly as they crossed Manhattan Bridge. The fog had lifted a little, but it was not yet daylight when Dale stopped before a large building. It loomed, gray and forbidding, against the cold night sky.

Inside, the scrubbed stone floors and bare walls gave Judy the impression that they had entered a fortress instead of a hospital. A uniformed guard at the door directed them to a desk where Judy learned that Peter had been taken to a private room in the new wing. The operation was over, but he was still under sedation, the nurse said. She added brightly, "You can see him in about an hour."

It would have been a long hour if another nurse, on night duty, hadn't suddenly recognized Irene. Irene had come in with Judy, leaving Dale to mind little Judy, who was asleep in the car.

"You're the Golden Girl, aren't you?" the nurse asked, stopping Irene as they entered the luxurious waiting room in the new wing. "One of our patients has been asking for you—"

"Clarissa!" Judy and Irene exclaimed in the same breath.

The nurse looked a little puzzled.

"We have to wait here anyway. Could we see her?" asked Irene. "We were awfully worried. Was she badly hurt? We looked all over the theater. How and where did it happen?"

"It was a street accident," replied the nurse in a brisk, professional manner. "She was in a cab. Her doctor can give you the details. I'm afraid you can't visit her at this hour. It would disturb the other patients. Except in extreme emergencies, visitors are never allowed before daylight."

CHAPTER XIV

Serious Trouble

JUDY wanted to tell the nurse that this was an extreme emergency. But was it? A girl had vanished. Still the fact remained that she might have slipped out of the theater on purpose.

"Peter will help us figure out what really happened," declared Judy. "Oh, I hope he's well enough to be—interested. Right now I'm more concerned with what happened to him."

"Will he be allowed to tell you?" Irene asked.

"I don't know. So much of his work is secret. That's the hardest part," Judy continued, a little break in her voice. "I never know what dangers he's facing. Usually he tries to make a joke of it when I ask him. But this time I can't help thinking—"

Irene's hand closed gently over Judy's. "Don't think

94

of what might have been. Just be glad he's here with good nurses to take care of him."

"I am glad. I'm glad Clarissa's here, too—if that patient is Clarissa. I'd like to think she didn't trick us, but how could the accident have happened?" Judy wondered. "And where was she going in a cab?"

"It almost makes a person believe in phantoms, doesn't it?" Irene asked. "Clarissa was so—naïve is the word. And now if she's hurt—Oh, Judy! Why are we always getting mixed up in other people's troubles? We have enough of our own."

"The way I look at it, other people's troubles are our troubles. Peter feels that way, too," Judy continued thoughtfully. "He says what hurts one of us hurts all the rest. We can't isolate ourselves and pretend trouble doesn't exist. We have to fight the good fight with fidelity, bravery, and integrity. That's the motto of the FBI, and if anybody has those three qualities, it's Peter. He's faithful, brave, and I never knew anybody as honest and sincere and—and—"

Judy was in tears, suddenly. The strain of waiting had been too much. A nurse, hurrying in, reassured her that Peter's condition was not serious.

"He is asking for you," she added in the usual composed manner of hospital nurses. "Will you come?"

Would she come? Judy wondered how she kept her feet from flying down the corridor. At the door of Peter's room she paused, a nameless fear coming over her.

"You go in first," she begged of the nurse, who had preceded her. "I'm not sure I look all right."

"You look fine," the nurse interrupted with a smile. "He's seen enough of me. It's you he wants. Go in to him just as you are, Mrs. Dobbs. I think it would be better if you went in alone."

Irene was quick to understand. "I'll go out and tell Dale—"

"Tell him not to wait," Judy said. "I'll be here all day. I'll come out to Long Island this evening—by train."

The slight hesitation in Judy's voice did not betray her. She dreaded that train ride. But she felt she had to take herself in hand. Peter was depending on her.

A hospital attendant spoke to Judy as she entered the large, cheerful room where Peter was lying flat in bed with a bottle of transparent liquid suspended above his bed. "Watch the intravenous. He mustn't move his arm."

"I understand," Judy replied. "My father is a doctor. I'll see that nothing goes wrong."

Her voice was determinedly cheerful. The young attendant left, closing the door softly. Judy was alone with Peter. For a moment she was all choked up with emotion and didn't know what to say. He smiled a little, wryly, and glanced toward the bottle that was feeding liquid nourishment into his veins.

"Careful there," he warned as she bent over to kiss him. "That's my breakfast there in the bottle. A funny way to eat!"

"I'll be careful," she promised. "I'll sit on the other side of the bed. Which shoulder was it?"

"The left."

"Then I'll sit on the right. You want me to stay here, don't you?"

"Yes, I want you." Peter's strong fingers closed over her outstretched hand. "Judy, it was my big chance, and I muffed it. I let him get away."

"Don't try to talk about it—unless you want to," Judy told him gently. "You're still very weak. You must save your strength."

"You're right." He was quiet for a moment just looking at Judy as if he could never see enough of her.

"You're always—so brave," he said at last.

Judy didn't feel very brave. She felt like bursting into tears again. Little by little she heard how Peter had been brought to the hospital unconscious from loss of blood. They had given him a transfusion before the operation. That was why it had taken so long. Removing the bullet, he said, was a simple matter. It had been imbedded in the flesh close to his shoulder blade.

"I'll be as good as new in a day or so," he assured Judy, who sat beside his bed, ready to listen whenever he felt like talking. "My partner cornered most of the gang. They were better organized than we thought. We trailed this man—"

"What man?" Judy asked when Peter paused.

"His name's Clarence Lawson. I can tell you about it now. It's public knowledge. The public has to be warned against such characters," he continued. "It all started when a woman came into our New York office and said her church had never received a donation she had given a man who claimed to be on the Ways and Means Committee. He'd enlisted her sympathy and talked her into donating quite a substantial sum to what she thought was the building fund. Lawson had joined the church and gained the confidence of a number of influential people."

"That's what you call the confidence game, isn't it?" asked Judy. "Did you catch up with this—this Lawson?"

"Well, almost. We trailed him and overheard some of his plans. Then we made some quick plans of our own. Did you ever hear the story of the three little pigs?"

"Of course," Judy replied, puzzled. "Are you joking? What do the three little pigs have to do with it?"

"The third pig, if you will remember, got to the orchard ahead of the wolf. Well," Peter continued, "that was what we planned to do. We were there, but the wolf was early, too. So he huffed and he puffed and he blew the house in, and he shot up the poor little pigs."

"Where was this house?" asked Judy. "Or aren't you allowed to tell?"

"I can tell you where it wasn't—" Peter sighed tiredly.

"No need," Judy told him gently. "Stay quiet for a while, and I'll tell you a story. We met a girl, and Pauline thinks she was playing the confidence game, too. Anyway, she made us sorry for her, and we each gave her five dollars so she could take the train home to West Virginia."

"Did she take it?"

"The train? I don't know. She took the money, if that's what you mean. She also accepted our invitation to Irene's show. I wish you could have seen it, Peter. Irene was marvelous as the good fairy, and her guest star, Francine Dow, made a beautiful Sleeping Beauty. The witch was a little frightening, though. She swooped in and seemed to cast an evil spell over the audience. Then Clarissa—"

"Clarissa?"

"She's the girl I was telling you about," Judy said. "She's here in the hospital, I think. Peter, would you like to rest while I find out if the patient they brought here really is Clarissa? If I speak to the nurse who recognized Irene, I'm sure they'll let me see her."

"Is Irene here?" Peter questioned, pain as well as puzzlement in his blue eyes as they searched Judy's face.

"She was. Oh, Peter! I hope I'm not tiring you, talking so much!" Judy exclaimed. "One of the nurses stopped Irene on the way in and said a patient had been asking for her. We thought of Clarissa right away. You see, if she met with an accident, it would explain her disappearance. I did tell you she vanished, didn't I? We never saw her leave the theater, but I suppose she could have slipped out during the show and afterwards changed her mind and tried to come back."

"She could have slipped out with no intention of coming back. I doubt if you'll find her here in the hospital," Peter said, "but it will do no harm to try.

I can see you're deep in another mystery. I wish I could help you solve it."

"You can, Peter. You'll be well soon," Judy told him hopefully. "Then we can help each other."

"I wish you wouldn't try to help me this time, Angel." Peter's voice was grave. "I'm in trouble—serious trouble, and I'd rather you kept out of it."

CHAPTER XV

The Wrong Girl

Just outside the door to Peter's room, Judy paused, trying to think. Serious trouble! What did Peter mean? Had the man, Lawson, the wolf in sheep's clothing, discovered his whereabouts? Would he be waiting for him when he was released from the hospital?

"Oh, please! Keep him safe," Judy said to the walls which seemed, suddenly, to move dizzily before her eyes. The activities of the hospital day were beginning. Night nurses were going off duty. Day nurses were busy with breakfast trays. Carts were being wheeled —up and down. Up and down. In a moment Judy feared she would find they were being wheeled by golden-haired nurses with identical faces.

"Do you feel faint?" a voice asked quietly.

Judy turned to see one of the nurses standing beside her. The dizzy feeling had passed.

"Thank you, nurse. I'm all right—now. I was looking for the night nurse, but I guess I'm too late. Could you direct me—to the patient who was asking for the Golden Girl?"

"The patient is awake," was the quiet answer. "But you must have a permission slip to see her. Tell the guard you think you can identify the patient in Room 334, and you will be allowed to go up."

"Oh!" exclaimed Judy, catching her breath in an exclamation of surprise. "Isn't she identified?"

"Not yet," the nurse replied. "She's in a semi-coma. Sometimes we can make a little sense out of what she says, and sometimes we can't."

"If she's Clarissa, I don't wonder. Didn't she give her name?"

"No, not her own name. All she would tell us was that she had to see Irene Meredith. Mrs. Meredith didn't leave, did she?"

"I'm afraid she did. But I know her. I can identify her."

"Good!" exclaimed the nurse. "The guard will probably let you go right up."

Five minutes later Judy was standing beside a bed with crib sides around it. The next thing she saw was a white face—white and wholly unfamiliar. Flaming red hair fanned out on the pillow. The woman looked at least thirty. Judy gazed at her a moment. Then she turned to the nurse who had escorted her to the room.

"I'm sorry," she said. "My friend, Clarissa Valentine, disappeared. I thought this patient might be Clarissa, but she isn't. I never saw her before in my life."

"Can't you tell me anything at all about her?" the nurse asked anxiously.

"Nothing except what you probably know already. We talked with the taxi driver after the ambulance drove away from the scene of the accident. He told us what little we know about it. Apparently this woman was on her way to the theater to see Irene's— I mean the Golden Girl show. I'm sorry," Judy finished.

"Sorry," mumbled the patient. "Everybody's sorry." Then, suddenly grasping the crib sides, she cried, "I've got to get out of here. Please, let me out."

"And then?" the nurse prompted Judy.

"Well, then we heard the ambulance siren. The show was nearly over so we waited until afterwards to find out what it was. That's all I know. I'm afraid it won't be of much help."

"No, I'm afraid not," the nurse replied sadly as Judy turned to go.

Peter was sleeping when she returned to his room. He looked so peaceful she decided not to awaken him. She'd help, though. Later on they'd talk it all over. There was sure to be some way she could help.

"I'll go out and have breakfast," Judy told the new nurse who had just come on duty. The day nurse assured her that there was no need for her to come back until visiting hours that afternoon.

"You'll notice a big change in your husband by

then. He will probably sleep most of the morning."
Judy tried to hide a yawn and the nurse added,
"You could use a little sleep yourself, Mrs. Dobbs.
You must have been awake most of the night."

Judy didn't say so, but she had rested more when
she was awake than when she had been dreaming.
What had caused those terrible nightmares? Judy
dreaded sleep because of them. She ordered two cups
of coffee in a nearby restaurant, hoping to keep herself awake. Then she telephoned Pauline Faulkner and
told her about Peter.

"You poor girl! Why don't you come up and rest
at my house until visiting hours?" Pauline suggested.
"I expect Flo. It's Sunday, or had you forgotten?"

"I do need some sleep," Judy admitted." But I keep
dreaming the same dream every time I close my eyes.
I'd never dare—"

"That's funny," Pauline interrupted. "So do I. And
just now when I spoke to Flo she said she'd had a
rough night, too. She didn't say why but, to use an
old expression of yours, I'd like to bet something
precious that it was because she had nightmares, too.
Come up and we'll compare notes. I feel—" Pauline
lowered her voice almost to a whisper. Judy could
hardly hear the word "bewitched," but she knew the
feeling.

When Judy arrived at the tall stone house which
was Dr. Faulkner's combined home and office, she
said, "Pauline, as you said, it's Sunday. Let's go to
church."

"All right." Pauline hesitated a moment. Then she said, "You may not like my church, Judy. It isn't at all like the one you attend."

"Which one?" asked Judy. "The little white church in Dry Brook Hollow isn't like the one I used to attend in Farringdon, but I like them both. I think it does a person good to learn different ways of believing, don't you? How is your church different, Pauline?"

Pauline shrugged. "I don't know. It's just a little more formal. But if you watch other people and do what they do you'll get along all right. The order of service is printed on the church calendar. They'll give you one as you come in. It's a little church crowded in between two tall buildings. They're going to tear it down and build a new one farther uptown. I'm rather sorry. But I guess it's best."

"In other words, you bow to the inevitable."

Pauline laughed. "You sound like your brother Horace. Does he know about Peter, Judy? It isn't going to be in the newspapers, is it?"

"I don't think so. Not yet, anyway. I telephoned home right after breakfast. Horace will put something in after he checks with the authorities. Publicity could be dangerous. That's what I told him. There's nothing about Peter in the New York papers. I did find this, though."

Judy pointed to a review of *Sleeping Beauty*. A columnist, known for his sarcasm, had called the play a triumph of youth over experience.

"As for the star, if that was Francine Dow, she

has certainly discovered the fountain of youth. She has lost her voice and gained the fragile beauty of a china doll. This reviewer couldn't believe his eyes."

"There are others like it," Pauline spoke up as Judy paused in her reading. "Here, I'll show you. This paper calls her a changeling."

"No?" Judy stared at the paper. "That's what Clarissa called herself. I don't get it at all. She was right beside us—"

"Was she?"

"I don't *know*. I certainly thought she was. Here's Flo. Maybe she can explain it," Judy finished as the doorbell rang.

CHAPTER XVI

The Name on the Calendar

FLO was flushed and excited.

"Have you seen the papers?" was her first question. "The reviewers don't think that was Francine Dow on Irene's show. They say—"

"We saw it," Pauline interrupted.

"But those were the very words Clarissa used. Is there any word from her?"

"Not yet. Perhaps there never will be. Peter says she could have slipped out of the theater with no intention of coming back. He's in the hospital, Flo. I'm so upset!"

"What happened to him?" Flo was immediately all sympathetic concern.

Judy started to tell her and then thought better of it. Florence Garner was a stranger, too. Judy had met her only a few hours before she met Clarissa. "I

107

shouldn't trust strangers," she told herself grimly. Aloud she said briefly, "He was hurt. He's in the same hospital where they took that redheaded woman. She was asking for Irene. I don't know why. We both thought she might be Clarissa—"

"But she wasn't? Then who is she?"

"She doesn't know," replied Judy. "It's all so confusing, I need a little peace and quiet to make any sense to what's happening. We thought we'd go to church."

Flo looked from one of them to the other.

"You're not telling me everything," she charged. "Something's happened. Something terrible has happened, and you're keeping it from me. Do you think dreams warn people of tragedy? I dreamed—It's still so real I can hardly tell you about it. But I dreamed that my hair—" She touched her head and seemed relieved upon discovering she was wearing her hat. "Well, never mind about that now."

"Clarissa hypnotized us. We're all under her spell. Maybe church—"

Judy stopped Pauline before she could finish.

"Religion isn't magic," she said quietly. "It's—something inside."

Judy's sudden sincerity seemed to confuse Flo.

"Well, I—I thought you were keeping something from me, but if you want me to go—"

"Of course we want you." Pauline decided the question for her. "Shall we go?"

Judy found Pauline's church even more formal than

she had described it. The minister and the people in the choir wore black robes. Judy's prayers were all for Peter and his work that had been so cruelly interrupted. Thoughts of what he must have suffered took possession of her mind and would not leave her.

"And so it is, my friends," the minister was saying, "we love each other and think that is enough. But were we not commanded in the fifth book of Moses, 'Love ye therefore the stranger; for ye were strangers in the land of Egypt.'"

Now Judy was more confused than ever. Clarissa was a stranger. Judy had followed her heart and loved her as a friend. But had she done the right thing? Was she a friend or a phantom? Should she have trusted her? What of the confidence game?

The words of the church service were printed on the calendar Judy had received at the door when the usher had handed her the hymnal. On the back, as she turned the calendar over in her hand during the long sermon, she noticed a list of names. Trustees of the church and the chairmen of various committees were listed. The names meant nothing to her until, all at once, she saw the name, *Clarence Lawson!* He was listed as chairman of the Ways and Means Committee. It seemed impossible. Could he, a man wanted by the FBI, be sitting quietly in the congregation? Peter had trailed him and lost him.

"Peter said it was public knowledge," Judy thought. "But surely these people don't know the name of a confidence man is printed on their church calendar!"

Pauline, sitting on her right, touched Judy's elbow. She was the last one to stand up when the congregation rose to sing the closing hymn. Flo gave her a look that asked, wordlessly, "What's the matter?" Pauline whispered something to Flo as they filed out of church, and Judy knew Pauline had told Flo that Peter had been shot.

"That's the name of the man he was trailing." Judy pointed to the name on the back of the calendar. "Do you know him?"

"Of course," Pauline replied, puzzled. "Everybody in the church knows him. He's conducting our building fund drive."

"Is he here?" asked Judy.

Pauline looked around. "I don't see him. That's funny. He never misses a Sunday. His wife isn't here either."

"Is she an actress?"

"Heavens, no! She's a typical clubwoman, if you know what I mean. They haven't been here long, but already she's at the head of everything. I don't know where she is this morning."

"She doesn't—have red hair, does she?"

"What are you thinking, Judy? Her hair is gray. If you're trying to identify that patient in the hospital you ought to ask Irene about her. They must know each other if she was asking for her. Maybe she's an actress. Irene knows a lot of theatrical people. Authors are my specialty," Pauline finished with a laugh.

"Ad men are mine. They would change the minister's text around to make it read, '*Sell* ye therefore the stranger,' but that's today's world," Flo said with a sigh. "Nobody cares much about the kind of love they tell you about in church."

"I care about it," Judy said.

Flo gave her an odd look. "You sound like Clarissa. She said she cared about the truth, but what happens? She disappears—with our money. I guess you just don't know what anybody is these days."

Pauline agreed. "The people in our church certainly don't know who Clarence Lawson is. Why was Peter trailing him, Judy? Is he wanted by the FBI?"

"Yes, he is. It's about some money for a church building fund. He was supposed to turn it over to the treasurer of the church, but he didn't."

"Didn't he? Oh dear!" Pauline exclaimed. "We didn't give much, because we weren't very enthusiastic about the new building, but a lot of people did. It's supposed to be a real community center when it's finished. Mr. Lawson knew an architect who drew up the plans and made an estimate. There was talk of bringing in professional fund raisers before Mr. Lawson took over. He said there was no need to pay people to raise money among us if we'd give it freely without pledges. Then he passed a plate around, and people threw in big bills and checks made out to him as chairman of the Ways and Means Committee. He talked people into giving just the way Clarissa did. He was like her in a way. Even his name is a little like hers—Clarence, Clarissa—"

"That's probably just a coincidence." In spite of the evidence against her, Judy found herself defending Clarissa. "It's the way I feel about her. I have no other reason," she admitted. "You girls are probably right."

CHAPTER XVII

A Wanted Thief

"Judy!" The exclamation came from Pauline, very suddenly as if she had just thought of something. "I know what we ought to do. We ought to visit Mr. Lawson. If he really is the thief I'd like to know about it. I could pretend I wanted to make a donation or something. Shall we try it?"

Judy hesitated. She didn't like that sort of pretending, though sometimes it was the best strategy. Also, Peter had asked her to stay out of trouble, and this would be walking right into it. But it could very easily be her chance to help him.

"How do we get there?" she asked. "Is it very far?"

"I'm hungry. Let's eat something first," Flo suggested.

The three girls had lunch in the same restaurant

where they first met Clarissa. They asked the cashier about her, but he claimed he remembered no such scene as they described.

"No one goes away from this restaurant angry," he told them. "Do you see that?" He pointed to a decorated sign bearing the words: OUR AIM IS TO PLEASE THE BEST PEOPLE IN THE WORLD, OUR CUSTOMERS.

"But this girl tried to cheat you," Pauline protested.

"She was a customer. She was still one of the best people," he replied without a change of expression.

"You might as well talk to a statue," Flo whispered. "Come on."

"It's only a few blocks to the house where Mr. Lawson lives," Pauline told them. "It isn't as cold and blustery today as it was yesterday. We can walk."

On the way, Judy and Flo began comparing their dreams of the night before.

"I know it sounds ridiculous," Judy said, "but I can't help feeling that my dream was a warning of some kind and that we ought to heed it. I'm not just sure how."

"What about you, Pauline? Did you dream about hair, too? That may be a clue to what's happening to us, if you did," Flo said eagerly.

The dark-haired girl shook her head. "My dreams are never very clear. I can't remember them well enough to tell them afterwards. I only know I cried out in my sleep, and Mary came up to see what was the matter. She said I was calling for my mother. I never do that. I hardly remember her. Mary's kept house for us ever since I was about little Judy's age. But Mother did have golden hair. I take after Father. I wish—"

"Don't say it," Judy stopped her. "You're going to wish you had golden hair."

"Could we have been hypnotized?" Flo began.

"I don't know. Ask your father about hypnotism, Pauline," Judy urged. "He'll know. He may use it on his patients. Dr. Zoller, a sort of uncle of mine, is a hypnotist, and Dad approves of it when it's not misused. Of course, if hypnotism was part of a confidence game Clarissa was playing—"

"It was! I'm sure of it," Flo interrupted. "She said we read her mind, and she talked us into buying that shampoo, didn't she?"

"I'm not sure. I thought it was your idea," Judy began.

"Well, I'm sure. She talked us into lending her the money, too. Then she left the theater when we were all so interested in the play we didn't notice. It was all a trick," declared Flo. "Can't you see it? Clarissa did it all."

"She even vanished on purpose," Pauline agreed. "It's clear to me—"

"It's clear to me, too," Judy interrupted. "It's perfectly clear that we haven't found out a single thing. Isn't it about time we started using our heads? Peter doesn't jump to conclusions without examining the evidence. If he's willing to risk his life to turn up a few facts to present at preliminary hearings, the least we can do is discuss this with him before we decide who's guilty."

"Guilty of what?" asked Flo. "Making us dream?"

Suddenly all three girls began to laugh. It seemed ridiculous for them to be taking their dreams so seriously. But their laughter died in their throats when they reached Mr. Lawson's house. Judy was the first to notice the shattered glass in the door. It was broken in a peculiar way. Several round holes with cracks radiating from them told the story.

"Bullet holes!" she exclaimed. "This was the place where it happened. You're too late, Pauline. You won't find Mr. Lawson—"

Meantime Flo had rung the bell. A heavy-set woman came in answer to it just in time to hear the name. She peered at the girls through the shattered glass before she opened the door.

"So it's Mr. Lawson you want, is it?" she inquired. "And what would you be wanting with the good man?"

Good man! Judy could hardly contain herself. Did the woman know what sort of man he really was? Or had he fooled her just as he had fooled the people in Pauline's church? He had even outwitted Peter.

"We did want to see him," Pauline began, affecting a timid voice. "We came to make a donation—"

"Indeed!" the woman interrupted. "I'll take it, if you please, and forward it to him. He's away for a couple of weeks."

"Far away," thought Judy, "and not likely to come back." Aloud she said, with perfect control, "We prefer to send the money ourselves. Could you give us his address?"

"Well, now, I could." She hesitated a moment and then went inside, returning with a piece of paper on which a post office box number was written. "You can reach him there," she said briefly and closed the door.

"Now what do we do?" asked Flo. "Shall we write him a letter and invite him to come back home and be arrested? We aren't really going to send him any money, are we?"

"He doesn't need our money. He has plenty," Judy began when Pauline interrupted heatedly.

"He certainly has. People were generous. There was all of fifty thousand dollars in the building fund. With that much on hand he can stay in hiding for a long, long time. Are you going to tell Peter where we were?" Pauline asked suddenly.

"Eventually," Judy said. "It bothers me when I have to keep things from him. He won't like it, of course. Maybe I ought to wait until he's feeling a little better before I say anything."

"I think you're right," Pauline agreed. "Just stay cheerful for Peter, and don't worry about a thing."

CHAPTER XVIII

Thieves of the Mind

JUDY found Pauline's advice hard to follow.

"Don't worry about a thing," she had said when they parted on Sunday. But the words had meant very little. In church, in the restaurant, in front of the bullet-riddled door, on the subway returning to the hospital, and especially on the train going back to Long Island—wherever Judy went a vague worry went with her.

"What's the matter with me?" she wondered. "Why can't I clear my head and think straight the way I used to?"

Judy spent a restless night, haunted by the faceless golden-haired people of her dream. Again she was looking for Clarissa. But now she had a clue. They had all dreamed about hair—Pauline, Flo, and herself.

But why? If they had been hypnotized as part of a confidence game, Peter ought to know about it. The next day Judy told him.

"You'd almost think someone had taken possession of our minds. All three of us had nightmares. What do you suppose caused them?" she asked when she was visiting him in the afternoon.

Peter shook his head. He was sitting up with his shoulder in a cast and feeling very much better. She hadn't wanted to tire him the day before. But now it was different. There were a number of things she knew she mustn't keep from him any longer.

"Nightmares are sometimes caused by something hidden in the subconscious mind," he replied. "I'm sure I don't know what you have hidden there."

"Oh, Peter! I'm not hiding it on purpose. I feel silly telling you about it after all you've been through," Judy burst out impulsively. "Will you forgive me?"

"On one condition," he told her.

Judy thought he was serious until she saw the twinkle in his eyes.

"And what is that condition?"

"That you tell me more. You told me yesterday that the patient you visited wasn't Clarissa, but you didn't tell me much of anything else. What happened to this phantom friend, as you call her?" Peter asked curiously. "Begin at the beginning and tell me exactly how you met her."

"We met her—in a restaurant. We went back there yesterday but didn't find out anything." Judy sighed.

It was good to be telling Peter about it. She had so much to tell him that she thought she might as well dish it out in small doses. The big surprise would come when she handed him the post office box number of the thief he had been trailing. But that could wait. She told him about church first, and how the minister had said, "Love ye therefore the stranger."

"It was easy to like Clarissa," she continued in answer to his first request. "You asked how we met her. Well, the four of us were having lunch when there was a commotion at the cashier's desk, and this stranger— we found out later that her name was Clarissa Valentine. Well, anyway, she claimed that she had given the cashier a twenty-dollar bill. He opened the cash drawer to prove that her bill wasn't in it, but she insisted and we believed her. Was that wrong, Peter?"

"Not at all," he replied. "I might have believed the girl myself and suspected the cashier of palming the bill."

"Then I'm glad we believed her. Not that it makes what happened afterwards any easier to explain," Judy added. "Pauline thought she had tricked us, but that was after she disappeared with the money we lent her. I don't know how she could have vanished the way she did if it wasn't a trick. Besides, the things she said—"

"What things?" asked Peter, more interested in the story than Judy had expected him to be. "If you can remember exactly what she said it may help us find out what happened to her."

"Oh dear, no! I'm afraid not. So much happened!

This is going to sound unbelievable to you," cried Judy, "but she said things that made it seem almost as if she—she didn't exist. Things like telling us she looked in a mirror once and saw no reflection. And then— you won't believe this at all, but when we toured Radio City and looked at ourselves on television, all the rest of us showed, but Clarissa was nothing but a big white light closing in until it disappeared just the way she did—without a trace. We called her a phantom friend for a joke at first, but after that it seemed so real it wasn't funny any more. Peter, what do you think happened?"

"Well, for one thing, a tube probably blew out on the TV set. That would cause the picture to close in and disappear. I've seen it happen myself, and it is weird—"

"It certainly was that," Judy agreed. "I suppose a tube could have blown out. We didn't wait to see what was wrong with the set, because Clarissa fainted. She wasn't faking, either. She was really frightened. We went back and saw ourselves after the set was fixed, but she wouldn't go near it. She said her hair was dull and drab and then we all started saying it— as if we were hypnotized or something. Was that a trick? Was Clarissa playing some sort of confidence game?"

"Someone was. I'll have to look into this myself," declared Peter. "It may tie in with what we found out. There are all kinds of thieves, you know. That cashier is probably a petty thief and should be reported. A thief like Clarence Lawson plays his confidence game for bigger winnings. But the most insidious kind, I think, are thieves of the mind. Do you follow me, Angel?"

"No, I'm afraid I don't," Judy admitted. "I've heard of brain washing, of course. I wish someone would wash those golden-haired people out of my brain, so I could stop dreaming about them and think straight. Is that what you mean?"

"I mean they may have been deliberately put there by the enemies of our most precious possession. You know what it is, don't you? It's our freedom to think our own thoughts."

"You mean—oh, Peter! I do see what you mean!" cried Judy. "I don't know how it was done, but someone has been doing things to our subconscious minds —to frighten us—and make us dream. Clarissa was frightened, too. She couldn't have done it. But who was it, Peter? How do we find out who did this horrible thing to us?"

"One way," said Peter, "is to review the facts. Judy, I'm serious. I want you to go back over everything that happened Saturday."

"But we've been doing that. We haven't come up with very many answers, only more questions. You said what happened to Clarissa might tie in with what you found out. What did you mean?" asked Judy.

"I told you we overheard some plans," Peter began. "Mind manipulation could have been part of them. If only we knew the name of the missing actress—"

"Is some actress missing? Maybe Irene knows her," Judy suggested. "She could give you the names of all the people who appeared on her show. There was the witch. She could have cast some sort of hypnotic spell over us, I suppose. Hypnotism is one sort of mind manipulation, isn't it?"

"Yes, but there are other sorts. There's a machine, for instance, called the tachistoscope. It's sort of a magic lantern with a high-speed shutter—"

"There were a lot of machines," Judy interrupted. "The studio floor was filled up with them. I tried to remember their names when we were on the tour, but I couldn't possibly remember them all."

"What else happened on that tour?" asked Peter. "You haven't told me everything."

"There's so much to tell. I can't think of it all at once. Irene invited Francine Dow to be her guest star. Did I tell you she didn't arrive until the last minute?" asked Judy. "Then she left hurriedly with her aunt before we had a chance to meet her."

"Did you meet the aunt?" Peter questioned. "A phony aunt would fit in very nicely with what we already know."

"What do you know? I can see you're not free to tell me," Judy added when Peter was silent. "But that doesn't mean I'm not free to think about it. These thieves of the mind may invent machines to make me dream, but when I'm awake I intend to do my own thinking, and right now I think Francine Dow may be in danger. She didn't sing. Irene thought she had a cold. But maybe something else was wrong. I didn't tell you, but there was an argument in the film storage room. The projectionist was very angry. I heard him say something might be as dangerous as an atom bomb. I had no idea what the danger was, but if Francine Dow is missing—"

Judy stopped. It wasn't Francine Dow, it was Clarissa Valentine who was missing. The two girls, as she remembered them, were somewhat alike. The absurd idea came to her that one of them could have been real and the other a changeling. But Peter didn't want fairy tales. He wanted facts.

CHAPTER XIX

Uncovering the Facts

"PETER," Judy said after a little silence, "you're looking for facts, and I do have something that may help you uncover them. It's—right here."

She handed him the slip of paper she had been saving and told him what it was.

"Lawson's post office box number!" exclaimed Peter. "I can't believe it. You should be working for us—"

"For you, Peter," she interrupted quietly.

"Where did you get this little piece of paper?"

"It was handed to me by a fat woman who peered at me from behind a shattered glass door—"

"Judy, you didn't—"

"I did," she confessed. "I found his name on the back of the church calendar, and Pauline told me where he lived. He was gone, of course. The people in the church don't know their building fund money went with him, do they?"

"They do now," Peter said, handing her the paper he had been reading when she came in. An item on the second page told only part of the story.

BOY HELD IN SHOOTING OF FBI AGENT PLEADS GUILTY IN KIDNAP PLOT, the headlines ran. Underneath it told how Frederick H. Christie, sixteen, of New York, arrested for the shooting of an FBI agent, pleaded guilty but refused to give any information that would lead to the apprehension of Clarence Lawson, who was wanted in a dozen states for extortion and robbery.

"Won't the box number I gave you lead to his apprehension?" asked Judy when she had finished reading the newspaper account.

"We can have the box watched. Maybe we can nab him when he comes for his mail. I'll be out of here in a day or two. Then we can really go to work on it. In the meantime perhaps we can uncover a few more facts. The so-called plot never got beyond the talking stage, the boy said. We may have scared them off. Since it didn't happen I guess I'm at liberty to tell you about it," Peter continued. "I think Lawson planned to bring the victim to his home and then changed his mind. We heard him say, 'We'll hold the actress until her husband comes across with a donation.' That's the way Lawson operates. His charities are all legitimate. People are asked to make donations on the theory that they may be helped because they have been helpers. Someone is missing. A donation is made, and the missing person promptly returns. It's one of the slickest ransom schemes anybody has yet devised. Somehow they work it so that the victim is never held against his will. Some worried relative donates money to a worthy cause. No law is broken until the money disappears. By then Lawson or one of his business partners is off for parts unknown. We would have nabbed him this time if bedlam hadn't broken loose in the street outside his house. It was staged to look like a rumble between two rival street gangs in which we were just accidentally involved."

"Oh, Peter!" exclaimed Judy. "Nobody will believe that."

"People do believe some surprising things. I'm no prophet," he said grimly, "but I predict the boys will get long sentences and Lawson will go scot free. It's happened that way before. He's one of the slickest criminals in the United States. I don't know who this actress was or how they planned to make her disappear, but they were counting on the fact that her husband would be worried."

"Her husband? Oh dear!" Judy exclaimed. "Irene is married. I ought to warn her—"

"No, please, don't alarm her," Peter interrupted. "It didn't happen the way they planned. I'm sure of that. It was supposed to take place Saturday night—"

"It was Saturday night that Clarissa disappeared. But she isn't an actress, and she isn't married."

"And she isn't a phantom," Peter added. "Whatever else we know about her, we can be perfectly sure she's real. She may be in real danger, too. If I can't find Lawson I want the confidence men who are working with him. This is no small outfit. It appears to be a nationwide organization. We want the top men, not just the tough kids they hire to do the shooting for them."

"Do you really think they were hired?" Judy asked.

"We know they were following orders. Their minds, in some way, had been taken over by the minds of the criminals who gave those orders."

"I see." Judy was quiet a moment. Did these mind manipulators have, in their possession, some fiendish machine more dangerous than an atom bomb? It was a terrifying thought.

"Peter," she asked, "what about Irene? Why didn't she have a nightmare like Pauline and Flo and me? Irene told me this morning that she hadn't dreamed an unpleasant thing."

"Was she on the tour with you?"

"No, she'd gone to her rehearsal. We didn't see her again until it was time for the show. There were a lot of people we didn't know on the tour with us," Judy remembered. "There was an ad man from Flo's office, too. He was the one who quarreled with Mr. Lenz."

"Mr. Lenz?"

"The projectionist. Irene's show isn't all live, you know. Sometimes they run film strips. Nearly all the commercials are on film. The show is sponsored by a tooth paste company now, but she's thinking of getting a new sponsor so she can be on one of the big networks. It would be almost like having her visit us every Saturday evening in our home. She was against it at first," Judy went on. "Flo asked me to talk her into it."

"Did you?"

"No. Irene knows what's right," declared Judy. "I still can't imagine her saying she uses a product when she doesn't. And she'd never use golden hair wash. She hates the idea of everybody being blond as much as I do. Imagine it, Peter! No more black or brown hair. No more dark blondes like Clarissa and Honey—"

"And no more redheads. We couldn't let *that* happen!" Peter exclaimed.

Judy gave him one of her special smiles. Gray eyes met blue ones in a moment of understanding. Then she said, "I want to help. I'll begin by making a list of the things we did Saturday."

"Ask Pauline and Flo to go over it with you," Peter suggested. "Then call up Irene. I would call her myself. They've given me a telephone right here at my bedside. But it would be better if you made the call from the booth outside."

"What'll I say? I'm so mixed up at this point I'm not sure what I'm trying to find out. Am I supposed to ask her about Clarissa or this unknown actress?"

"You're trying to find out about that redheaded patient upstairs, for one thing," Peter told her. "Ask Irene to come in and pay her a visit. She may know who she is."

CHAPTER XX

Identified

Judy's list, when she finally had it completed, was as long as Santa's list of good boys and girls. That was what she told Peter when she presented it to him.

"Pauline and Flo helped me. We put in everything we could think of in the order it all happened. But still I have a feeling there's something important that we left out. Irene's coming this evening," Judy added hopefully. "Maybe she has something to add to the list."

Much later, when Peter was being interviewed by one of the agents from the New York office and Judy had stepped outside his room for a moment, she almost bumped into Irene. For a moment they stared at each other. Then both of them said, in the same breath, "You're here!"

"Dale's here, too," Irene told her. "He's outside in the waiting room with little Judy. We'll take turns minding her so both of us can visit Peter."

"You'll have to wait. He has a visitor. Very confidential," Judy said, lowering her voice. "They're looking over a list that I gave them. Nobody is allowed in there until they've finished exchanging top secrets."

"Then I'll go up and visit Clarissa and find out what happened—"

"Wait, Irene!" Judy stopped her. "I should have told you. That patient isn't Clarissa. I don't know who she is, but you may be able to identify her. She keeps calling for you."

Irene looked her disappointment.

"She could be someone who's seen me on television —someone I don't know at all. Doesn't she know who she is?"

"I'm afraid not."

"Is she out of her head? I've never been able to overcome my fear of people who weren't—rational," Irene confessed. "Couldn't someone else identify her?"

"She wants you, Irene. She keeps asking for the Golden Girl. She was hurt on the way to see your show, and the idea seems fixed in her mind. She may calm down the minute she sees you," Judy said.

"I hope so." Irene paused, glancing back toward Peter's room. His visitor, portfolio in hand, had just come out. "We can go in now," she told Judy. "I'd rather not visit that woman upstairs until I've seen Peter."

"Wait a moment, Mr. Blake!" Peter called from his room. "Here are a couple of young ladies I want you to meet. They may have something to add to that list I just gave you."

He introduced the man to Judy and Irene. They greeted him cordially, and then Judy said, "I have nothing to add, Mr. Blake. If anything else happened I can't think of it, but Mrs. Meredith may have something for you. She's on her way to identify that red-haired woman who was hurt in the taxicab."

"I am going up, but I probably won't know her from Adam," Irene said.

"From Eve," Peter corrected her with a boyish grin. "Is Dale here? Maybe he might have a clue to her identity."

"If I had somebody to mind the baby in the waiting room, we could both go up," Irene began.

"I'll mind her," Judy said. "Is it all right, Peter? I won't be long."

"Of course it's all right. I'll go with you," Peter surprised Judy by saying. "I'm supposed to walk around and get used to this cast. It makes me feel a little top-heavy right now. You'll have to help me on with my robe."

Judy smiled. It was so good to see Peter up and walking. She escorted him to the waiting room where little Judy had to be stopped from pouncing on him. The baby stared at the cast and then said sorrowfully, "Peter all broke."

"How does she mean that?" asked Dale. "Good to see you so chipper," he added, shaking the hand that

Peter extended. "I've always heard that you can't keep a good man down."

Mr. Blake was introduced and invited to accompany Dale and Irene to the room in the old building where the red-haired woman was. They left quietly just as Peter was saying to little Judy, "I guess I must look something like a broken dolly to you."

"Baby," little Judy corrected him. Irene had brought along one of little Judy's "babies" to keep her amused.

"A dolly can also be a truck used for television cameras," Judy remarked. "You learn a whole new language. A chair becomes a prop, and a log is no longer something to throw in the fireplace. It's a complete record of everything that happens on a station from sign-on in the morning to sign-off at midnight. I might remember what I forgot to put on that list if I looked at the station log."

"Do that," advised Peter. "There may have been something to make you dream—"

"On television?" Judy laughed. "I don't know what it was unless that witch gave me nightmares."

"Funny witch!" spoke up little Judy.

"You see," Judy pointed out, "she was a funny witch. She wasn't frightening even to a baby. The whole play was delightful. Did you see the reviews of it? Nobody seemed to recognize Francine Dow. Little Judy is holding the doll—excuse me, I mean the baby, that played the part of Sleeping Beauty during the first part of the show. They also used a film strip of a real baby."

"The advertising was on film, too, wasn't it? That's one thing you did omit from your list," Peter pointed out. "You forgot to list the commercials you watched."

"The commercials! Who could list them? There are so many of them. Anyway, they aren't important. But maybe they are," Judy quickly amended her first statement. "That golden hair wash commercial started us worrying about our hair. We watched it when we were waiting for the tour to begin."

"At Radio City?"

"Yes, but it didn't originate from there. It was on a local channel. You know, the same one that features the Golden Girl show. I wish you could have been there, Peter."

"Perhaps that's where I should have been. There are federal controls to keep advertisers in line. If I had known—"

"Where Mommy Daddy gone?" little Judy interrupted, suddenly realizing that Dale and Irene were no longer in the room.

"They went to call on a patient," Judy explained hurriedly. She was eager to hear the rest of what Peter had started to say, but again the baby interrupted.

"Wanna see patient!"

"I'm a patient. You're visiting me," Peter told her.

"You're not sick," she replied. "You're mended."

"Beautifully mended," Peter agreed, kissing the top of her curly head. "It's no use, Judy. We'll have to explore the possibilities another time."

Little Judy chattered on. Peter let her examine his cast. "It's *hard*. Who did 'at? Scribbles on it," she observed.

"Autographs," Peter corrected her.

She tried to say the word and made such a funny *o* with her mouth that both Judy and Peter had to laugh. It wasn't easy for a two-year-old to say a big word like *autograph*. Any attempt at serious conversation was abandoned. All three of them were laughing and saying funny words when Dale and Irene returned. Mr. Blake was with them. They looked so serious that even little Judy stopped laughing.

"What's wrong?" Judy asked at once. "Did you know the patient? Is she all right?"

"She's—she's— Oh, Judy! I can't believe it," Irene burst out. "She must have been hurt right after the show."

"No, Irene. It was during the show." Judy remembered it distinctly. "We heard the ambulance siren right after Sleeping Beauty pricked her finger on the spindle and the witch pronounced the curse."

"Francine Dow played the part of Sleeping Beauty, didn't she?" Peter inquired.

"I certainly thought she did," Judy began.

"But that's impossible," Dale blurted out when Irene could only gasp in disbelief.

"You see," Mr. Blake pointed out, "we identified the patient. She's better. She knows her own name, and Mrs. Meredith is sure of it. *She is Francine Dow!*"

CHAPTER XXI

Explained

THE silence that followed Mr. Blake's announcement was like the moment after lightning strikes, when a clap of thunder is expected. It would come with the whole explanation. But at first Judy couldn't believe it.

"I don't understand this at all," she heard herself saying. "You couldn't have made a mistake, Irene?"

"No, Judy. Irene identified her. There's no mistake unless Clarence Lawson made it when he snatched the wrong girl. Do you think that could be what happened?" Peter asked the other FBI agent.

"It's worth an investigation," Mr. Blake replied. "This woman is Francine Dow all right. She was on her way to the theater when she was hurt."

"Do you mean—you can't mean that she never arrived! Then who was that up there on the stage? Someone played the part of Sleeping Beauty. Did you know it wasn't the guest star you invited?" Judy asked, turning to Irene in bewilderment.

"No, I didn't," she admitted. "I did think she'd kept her youth and beauty amazingly. But the right make-up can make a person look very young. I couldn't see what was going on backstage from where I was standing. Afterwards, when I saw the reviews, I suspected there had been a last-minute substitute. But I still don't know who she was."

"Doesn't anybody know?"

"The substitute does. Whoever she was, she played the part beautifully except for the last song. I did wonder why she didn't sing. There was an unscheduled wait when the witch was spinning," Irene said, "but I never guessed Francine Dow wasn't there. The show would have been ruined if someone hadn't stepped in to play the part."

"But who was that someone?" Judy wanted to know. "And how did she know the lines?"

"There were cards," Irene explained. "Cards are often used to prompt busy stars. Francine missed the rehearsals so we had the cards ready for her. The man on the dolly held them up."

"Baby," little Judy corrected Irene drowsily from Dale's arms, and promptly fell asleep.

"I wish I could sleep like that without dreaming," Judy said with a sigh. "My dreams are so real I keep thinking things that are actually happening are part of them. If I could only think—"

"You did all right when you compiled that list your husband showed me. That shows some pretty clear thinking," Mr. Blake complimented her.

"But this! If I could think back to the exact time—"

"That's it!" exclaimed Peter. "Now you're on the right track."

"Am I? It doesn't seem possible. But if the lines Francine had to say were on the cards, and the wig and costume were ready, it *could* have been played by some other actress. But who was she? Who took the part of Sleeping Beauty?"

"We know it wasn't Francine Dow," Irene said thoughtfully. "It wasn't one of the fairies. They were still in costume. I don't see who it could have been unless—"

She paused, and Peter said one word:

"*Clarissa!*"

"You're right, Peter!"

This was the clap of thunder Judy had been expecting. Somewhere in the back of her mind she had known it all along. Clarissa, in the golden wig and the princess costume, had shown her real beauty for everyone to see. There could have been no doubt, even in her own mind, that she was a vision of loveliness on TV.

"She said she'd do anything to get on television," Judy remembered. "Could she have planned all this?"

"I don't see how she could," Irene replied. "Nobody possibly could have known Francine Dow would have an accident. The whole show could have been spoiled!"

"But it wasn't. Clarissa played the part so well that everybody thought she was Francine Dow. But what happened afterwards?" asked Judy. "Francine's aunt must have known she wasn't the real Francine—"

"*If* that woman was her aunt," Peter put in, and suddenly, just as the realization had come that Clarissa had played the part of Sleeping Beauty, a new and more terrifying fact became apparent.

"Peter!" cried Judy. "Those plans to hold an actress until her husband gave a 'donation' were meant for Francine Dow. But if they're holding Clarissa—"

She stopped, aghast at the thought of what terror the girl, so easily frightened, must be feeling in the hands of Clarence Lawson and his ring of criminals. They had been desperate enough to use bullets to keep their plans from being discovered. Peter was aware of the danger.

"We must proceed with caution," he told Mr. Blake. "It's our job to see that the girl isn't hurt—"

"And that she's returned to her own people," his partner added. "Where can we get hold of them?"

That proved to be the big question. A minister somewhere in West Virginia was pretty vague. But it was enough to trigger the field office there into action. An ordained minister by the name of Valentine ought not to be hard to find.

Mr. Blake was ready to leave. He said he would get back to the office and set the machinery in motion. Meantime Peter decided to call up Washington, since every case investigated in the field had to be supervised and coordinated from FBI headquarters there.

"We'll get fast action on this," he promised a short time later, returning from the telephone booth just outside the waiting room.

Judy could see how difficult it was for him to move about with the heavy cast on his shoulder, but the urgency of his case seemed to give him new strength. She turned to Irene, who still seemed a little baffled by all that was happening, and said, "Poor Peter! I know how much he wants to get out there in the field, as he calls it, and do the investigating himself, but he can't. We mustn't let him try until he's stronger."

"Is Clarissa in danger? I don't understand what's going on at all," Irene admitted.

"None of us do. But we have to find out. There seems to have been a plot to kidnap some actress. It sounds like something out of one of my stories," Dale said, "but I'm afraid it's only too real."

He glanced at the sleeping baby he was holding, and Judy knew what he was thinking. Until Clarence Lawson and his ring of criminals were caught, none of them could be sure who his next victim would be.

"Peter's afraid they've snatched Clarissa, thinking she was Francine Dow. I don't know how a thing like that could happen. Why would she have gone with them without a protest? Let's go back over everything that happened," Judy suggested. "Mr. Lenz knows something—"

"You can't blame him for anything. He's the kindest, best man," Irene began to defend him.

"I'm not questioning his character," Judy told her. "I'm just remembering what he said. Something in that film storage room was dangerous. 'As dangerous as an atom bomb,' he said, and I think that something, whatever it is, may be a clue to what happened to Clarissa."

"What about Francine Dow? Why wasn't she reported missing? Didn't anybody care about her? She has a husband. She does try to conceal her age. She used to look a lot like Clarissa when she was a movie star. Now, with her hair dyed that weird shade of red and her face—Judy, it was a yellowish color. She looked terrible. I asked the nurse and she said Francine is in bad shape. I guess it's something pretty serious," Irene finished.

"And worry never helps. I've heard Dad say that," Judy remembered.

"I tried to tell her the show wasn't spoiled. It did quiet her a little," Irene said. "I suppose, now that they know who she is, the hospital will get in touch with her husband. Everything is out of our hands, Judy. We may as well go home and get a little rest."

Judy hoped she could rest without a whole parade of faceless golden-haired people swarming in to haunt her dreams. Flo had dreamed. So had Pauline. But what of Clarissa? Was there really something in that golden hair wash commercial to make them dream?

"You started to tell me something, Peter," Judy began. "You said there were federal controls to keep advertisers in line—"

"There aren't enough, I'm afraid. The big networks have banned this kind of advertising, but some of the local channels may be using it," Peter said.

"Advertising? But Mr. Lenz said, 'as dangerous as an atom bomb,' " Judy objected. "I thought he was talking about something that might blow up in our faces."

"Mind control is equally dangerous. Think about it," Peter advised. "Talk with this projectionist if you have a chance. We want to know exactly what you four girls saw on television."

CHAPTER XXII

Real Phantoms

"So THESE are our suspects?" Judy looked about at the array of machinery in the area just in front of the studio floor. It was the next day. She had come with Irene to rehearsal. To all appearances she was simply an interested friend, but Mr. Lenz knew, the moment he saw her, that she had come for another purpose.

"I've seen the papers," he said to Irene. "I know your friend is missing, and I can tell you something about what happened backstage last Saturday. I was standing at the door to the film storage room and saw it all. She came back here during intermission. Your guest star hadn't arrived, and everybody was all excited. When they saw this girl you call Clarissa Valentine they jumped to the conclusion that she was

Francine Dow and brought out the wig and costume."

"I see." It was clear to Judy what had happened. "Clarissa said she came to New York hoping to get a little part on TV. That was the way she put it. The part she got wasn't so little."

"She was there when she was needed," Irene put in, "but how did she happen to go backstage in the first place?"

"I think I can answer that question," Judy said. "She went back for those two bottles of shampoo she left in the dressing room, and when she saw Francine Dow wasn't there, she stepped into the part because she didn't want the show spoiled and because—well, it does happen that sometimes one person's failure is another's opportunity."

"I guess that's the way of it," agreed Mr. Lenz. "That girl can really act. With all the publicity she'll get when she is located, she's sure to be in demand, and I don't mean just for spot advertising."

"Speaking of advertising," Judy began as if it had just come up casually in the conversation, "there was a commercial on this channel last Saturday—"

"If you mean the golden hair wash commercial, it won't be shown again. I can promise you that," the projectionist went on, becoming excited. "I know why you've come. I could see you were curious. Well, that young ad man had talked somebody here into showing that film, phantoms and all—"

"Phantoms?" The word burst from Judy's lips. "What phantoms, Mr. Lenz?"

"That," said Mr. Lenz, perching on his counter

like an angry bird, "will take a little explaining." He waved his hand toward the pigeonholes behind him, where rows upon rows of film were stored for future use on the program. "It's my job to bring the contents of those cans to life. There's everything there—spot commercials, feature films, half-hour shows—everything. People who watch these films know what they're watching. If they don't like the program they can turn it off. If the commercial displeases them they can always walk out of the room until it's over.

"But here," he went on, "is something being fed into your mind without your knowledge and without your consent. You can't turn it off because you don't know you're watching it until, suddenly, you feel compelled to buy some product or, worse yet, you're plagued with guilt because you didn't buy it. This is called subliminal advertising, and it's forbidden—just as it should be. Only once has it been used on this channel—"

"Was that last Saturday, Mr. Lenz? Was it shown on Teen Time Party?"

"Yes. Superimposed on the picture of the golden-haired girl you saw was another picture—a shadowy, faceless figure which the advertiser wished you to imagine was yourself. This phantom was flashed on the screen too fast for your conscious mind to be aware of it. But your subconscious mind recorded it. And a desire was planted. You began to want to be like the beautiful golden-haired girl rather than the faceless shadow."

"I dreamed of faceless people," cried Judy. "They

had golden hair, and they were all alike. They frightened me, Mr. Lenz. I couldn't get them out of my mind."

"Did you associate them with such words as *drab* and *dull?*" he asked.

"That's what Clarissa kept saying about her hair. I thought—we all thought she'd hypnotized us in some way. Why? Were those words flashed on television, too? Were all those queer feelings we couldn't explain the result of that program we watched?"

"I'm afraid they were, my dear. But the film will not be shown again. I can promise you that. Erase it from your memory, if you can. But remember! Those faceless phantoms could be real if we once lost our freedom to think!"

He stopped, as if spent by his outburst, and Irene said, "We'll remember, won't we, Judy? This has certainly been a lesson for me."

"What do you mean, Irene?" asked Judy.

"Because I'd just about decided to do the golden hair wash commercial. That is, I thought if Clarissa used the stuff, she could do the commercial for me. And with all the publicity she'll be getting, people will be eager to see her. But now that I know that sponsor uses subliminal advertising, I wouldn't think of working for those people," Irene exclaimed.

"What's more, Mrs. Meredith," Mr. Lenz observed, "if the golden hair wash people don't give up the use of subliminal advertising, no major network will have anything to do with them."

"That's right," Irene sighed. "And I did so want to

be on one of the big networks. It isn't just the extra money. It's being able to entertain so many more people—especially you," she confided with a fond look at Judy. "You won't see me on your TV at home until I do."

"It's a shame," Judy sympathized. "But you'll get there sooner or later. And when you do, I hope you'll repeat *Sleeping Beauty*."

"I'd like to," Irene said, "but how can I unless we find Clarissa?"

Judy shook her head. "We haven't anything, not even a picture of her for the papers, and so far they haven't been able to locate any minister named Valentine in West Virginia. Peter says it's probably not her real name."

"You'll find her," Mr. Lenz said. "But if she goes on the air for golden hair wash, she'll be giving up more than she can possibly gain."

"Peter said there were thieves of the mind," Judy said, "and I'm beginning to understand what he meant. You wouldn't know it if they flashed those faceless phantoms on a film you had made. It would be their film, wouldn't it? They could do that—"

"Not without warning the viewers," Mr. Lenz interrupted. "The public does have that much protection. The technique has been used in horror films, but the viewers have been warned."

"Warned of what?" asked Judy. "Were they told that the film would give them nightmares?"

"Yes. As I told that young ad man, it's still in the experimental stage. It's dangerous—"

"As dangerous as an atom bomb. That's what you said," Judy reminded him.

"And that," declared the projectionist, "is exactly what I meant. The day a man's thinking can be controlled without his knowledge will be the day that marks the end of freedom."

"No!" cried Judy. "We won't let that happen!"

Mr. Lenz gave Judy's hand such a grip that she winced, but afterwards it was good to remember. And there were no more nightmares, for Judy at least. After she had talked it over with Peter she knew exactly what had happened and what they had yet to do.

CHAPTER XXIII

A Curious Letter

SHORTLY after Peter was discharged from the hospital, a letter came, addressed to Irene and post-marked Roulsville. It bore no return address.

"That's funny. It was forwarded to me from the studio," Irene said, turning it over in her hand. "My show is on a local channel. I don't have any fans in Roulsville."

"You know some people there, don't you?" Judy asked.

Irene shook her head. "Only you and your family. But they live in Farringdon."

"Horace could have been driving through Roulsville," Judy said, "but it isn't his handwriting. Anyway, he usually types—"

Peter interrupted, his blue eyes twinkling.

"The best way to find out who the letter is from is to open it," he suggested.

Dale laughed. "Why make such a mystery out of an ordinary letter?"

"Did you say an ordinary letter? This isn't—it can't be, but it is!" Irene exclaimed as she tore open the envelope.

"You aren't making any sense," Judy began.

"Does this make sense?" Irene waved four crisp five-dollar bills before her face. "Clarissa sent them! She returned our money. Oh, Judy! I can't believe it!"

"I can't either," Judy agreed. "How does Clarissa happen to be in Roulsville?"

"Wait till I read the letter," Irene said. "It's directed to all four of us."

Judy's bewilderment grew as Irene read:

"Dear Irene, Judy, Flo, and Pauline:

Enclosed are four five-dollar bills. Thank you for helping me, a perfect stranger. Do good and gain good, my father always says. Trust people and you will be trusted. Please tell the police and the FBI that I am safe at home and they can stop looking for me. I saw it all in the papers. Dad thinks I ought to give up the idea of a career on TV until I've finished high school here in Roulsville. I am sorry I had to leave the theater in such a hurry, but Francine Dow's aunt mistook me for her. I convinced her of her mistake and went home only to find that my parents were moving. I told you Dad used to be a minister, didn't I? He doesn't have a pastorate at present, but hopes to become active in church work. What church do you attend, Judy? I remember hearing you say you lived somewhere in the vicinity of Roulsville. We've bought a beautiful home here . . ."

"I'll bet they have," Peter commented, reading over Irene's shoulder. "Clarence Lawson has enough cash to buy a real beaut—"

"Clarence Lawson!" exclaimed Judy. "What are you saying, Peter? Clarissa's with her father."

"So the letter says. But did Clarissa write it?"

"It does sound a little stilted," Judy admitted. "And I'm not familiar with her handwriting."

"Well, I am familiar with some of those sayings she attributes to her father. *Do good and gain good*, for instance. Lawson's overworked that one. Those were the very words he used when he approached Francine Dow's husband for a donation. Dow and Francine had quarreled over her comeback on TV, and she'd left him to live with an aunt who had just come east from California."

"Did you interview the aunt?" asked Dale. "Or aren't you at liberty to say?"

"I didn't. I checked with our field office there. The real aunt is still in California. Lawson had found out about her, some way. The 'aunt' who called at the stage door and left with Clarissa really did mistake her for Francine Dow. That's one fact that is straight in the letter."

"But the others? She says she's living with her parents in Roulsville. Aren't these people really her parents? It is odd she didn't mention her brothers and sisters. Didn't she say she was one of six children?" Judy asked.

"I didn't hear her say that. I didn't hear her say a lot of the queer things you girls said she said when you were on that tour of Radio City," Irene replied. "I didn't hear her call herself a changeling, for instance, or say she looked in the mirror and saw no reflection. Maybe she is trying to trick us after all."

"It isn't Clarissa. It's Lawson who's trying to trick us," declared Peter, "but this time he won't get away with it. He's picked you for a sucker because you lent money to a stranger. I can't wait to see the look on his face when he finds out who you really are, Angel."

"You mean when he finds out I'm married to an FBI man," Judy laughed. "Peter, when can we leave for home?"

They had planned to return to Pennsylvania in a day or two, anyway. The letter made their return more urgent.

"Let's leave tomorrow morning," Peter suggested. "Maybe you'd better call your mother and ask her to open up the house. Otherwise it will be pretty cold. And I'm afraid you'll have to do most of the driving."

The Beetle had come through the gun battle with one small dent in its fender. That was repaired, and the car now looked like new. A few telephone calls were made and then the packing began. The following morning, Judy and Peter were on their way home.

"I don't like New York much," Judy admitted when they were out of the city, "especially Madison Avenue and what Flo calls the rat race to get a monopoly on all the big accounts. I don't want anything big. I guess I'm just a country girl at heart."

"My love for you is as big as all outdoors," declared Peter. "Don't you want that?"

The car went into a wild skid. Judy righted it and said, "There! Of course I want your love, but from now on I'm paying strict attention to my driving. All outdoors is pretty big this morning. We have three hundred miles of icy roads ahead of us with who knows what at the other end. Peter, take care this time, won't you? Please don't be alone when you meet Clarence Lawson."

He promised that he wouldn't be alone. He had seen to that. He also told Judy he would soon be leaving for Washington. "I need that refresher course. A fellow has to keep in training to be able to defend himself against such men," he said grimly. "I know how Lawson works, but I want to be prepared for his little surprises."

"How does he work?" asked Judy.

"He makes people like him for one thing. He looks and acts like a perfect gentleman. He and his wife are just the type of people you expect to see in church on a Sunday morning. With a lovely young 'daughter' like Clarissa to cover up for him, nobody will believe he isn't the real Pastor Valentine. He may get himself elected treasurer of the church as he did some years ago when he was known as David Barnes. I see what his plans are all right, but this time," Peter said with a determined look on his face, "we're going to nip them right in the bud. It's too bad Clarissa didn't put her street address on that letter."

"Roulsville isn't so big. Can't you check with the real estate office and find out who's bought property?"

"That's the usual procedure," agreed Peter. "I'll check with the churches, too. We'll find him if I have to canvass every house. It looks as if this case is going to wind up fast. Roulsville, of all places! Lady Luck has certainly smiled on us for once."

"Was it Lady Luck or good clear thinking on Clarissa's part?" asked Judy. "She didn't say what she meant in that letter, but I could read between the lines. I know your work is secret and I shouldn't talk about it, but if Clarissa did happen to overhear our conversation in the restaurant she may know you're with the FBI. That letter could be her way of asking for help without arousing the suspicions of her so-called parents."

"You're right, Angel. Clarissa isn't the only one who's been doing some good clear thinking," declared Peter. "Your nightmares haven't affected your thought processes in the daytime."

"I don't have them any more. I wonder . . ."

Judy's wonderings went on for mile after mile of uninterrupted driving. Were things falling into place too neatly? Certainly someone had planned this. Could it be Clarence Lawson himself? Had he dictated that letter and forced Clarissa to write it?

As they neared home Peter expressed what Judy had been thinking. "I wonder what Lawson is up to this time," he said. "Does he really think Clarissa will keep on pretending to be his daughter? He may have threatened her into leading us right into his trap."

CHAPTER XXIV

Trapped!

WITH Judy still at the wheel, the Beetle crawled down the last hill and into the valley that held the small city of Farringdon. They stopped at Dr. Bolton's house on Grove Street only to find it deserted.

"Mother may have gone over to Dry Brook Hollow to get our house ready for us, but Dad should be here. He has office hours from six to eight in the evening," Judy said in a worried voice, "and it's almost six o'clock now."

"We made good time. You must be tired. Let's drive right home to Dry Brook Hollow," Peter suggested. "Someone is sure to be there. Tomorrow I'll report at the resident agency and get my assignment. Lawson knows me. The SAC may want someone else to do the footwork."

The SAC, Judy knew, was the Supervising Agent in charge of the nearest field office. There were fifty or more such offices scattered throughout the country, and every one of them had been advised to be on the lookout for Clarence Lawson as well as for Clarissa. In the smaller cities surrounding the field offices the men worked out of resident agencies like the one recently set up in Farringdon, but they were still responsible to the SAC who, in turn, was responsible to the chief himself. It awed Judy when she thought of all the complicated machinery that had been set in motion to see that no harm came to one girl. It made her proud, too, that Peter was part of it.

"Would you mind?" she asked him as they drove on over the next hill and down into Dry Brook Hollow. "I mean, would you mind very much if David Trent or some other more experienced agent got the assignment?"

"A little," Peter admitted. "I'd rather like to bring Lawson in myself. If only he hasn't used Clarissa as bait for a trap—"

"Oh, Peter! That's what I've been thinking. Could it be—mind control? There seem to be so many ways of doing it. There's brain washing, and hypnotic suggestion, and high-pressure selling, and all the frightening new inventions for getting ideas into a person's subconscious mind without his knowledge or consent. It scares me when I think of the possibilities—"

"There are possibilities for good as well as evil," Peter told her. "Another type of mind control has

been used to reform prisoners, and it seems to work.
Their pillows talk to them—"

"What do you mean?" asked Judy. "Oh—" she
interrupted herself, "there's a man turning down our
road. Maybe it's just as well he didn't see us."

"We can drive down the North Hollow road, take
that short-cut through the woods, and head him off.
Want to?" asked Peter.

"It seems silly," she admitted, "but I think I do
want to. Look, Peter!" Judy exclaimed a few minutes
later, as she stopped the car and they both climbed
out. "Someone's broken a path through here. It should
be easy to head him off. I'll run ahead and meet him
before he gets to the bridge."

"Wait!" Peter called, but Judy was already running.
As she passed her house she thought she heard someone else call to her. Lights blazed from almost every
window, so she knew her mother must be there.

Just before she reached the bridge Judy slowed
down and caught her breath before she approached
the oncoming stranger. He was taking his time, apparently in no hurry to reach the house.

"Hi!" Judy called out bravely. "Are you on your
way to our house?"

"Greetings and salutations!" said the stranger, bowing politely. "I'm Pastor Valentine. You must be
Judy. My daughter, Clarissa, has invited me to your
party. I believe you know her."

"Yes, I know her," Judy said, "but I'm not giving
a party. Or am I?"

For a moment she almost believed the man was the real Pastor Valentine. But in the next moment the terrifying realization swept over her. He was Clarence Lawson! She smiled at him, trying to conceal her terror.

"It must be a surprise party. Well, I'm—surprised. I'll walk the rest of the way with you, Pastor Valentine, and introduce you to my guests."

She didn't ask if Clarissa was among them. She could only hope Peter had reached the house in time to telephone for help. The man, walking beside her, was the picture of gentlemanly dignity until, suddenly, a black shape darted in front of them.

"What's that?" he exclaimed, losing a little of his dignity.

"It's my cat. Don't you like cats, Mr. Law—I mean Pastor Valentine?"

Judy had let the name slip out. She could have bitten her tongue for it. The man dropped his polite mask and snarled, "I hate cats. They're unlucky, especially black ones."

It was a temptation to tell him that this particular black cat was unlucky only for criminals, but Judy resisted the urge as Lawson, recovering his poise, turned and said, "I'm sorry for the outburst, but I'm allergic to cats."

"My cat's the same way," Judy retorted. "He's allergic to some people."

"My dear! You will never make friends saying things like that. We do want to be friendly, don't we?"

he asked in placating tones. "After all, I am the father of a young lady who seems very fond of you."

"Is she?" asked Judy. "Then perhaps you can tell me where the young lady is."

"She's with her mother," was his clipped answer. "Now, if you will excuse me, I must be going—"

"Aren't you coming to my party? You must live near here," Judy ventured. "I notice you were walking."

"Good for the constitution," he replied and began to walk away more swiftly.

"Wait!" cried Judy. She couldn't let him escape. It had been a mistake to run and meet him in the first place. And she should never have spoken to him in the way she did. Now he was nearly to the bridge. Should she turn back or follow him and try to persuade him to return?

Judy had forgotten, for the moment, that Peter was part of an organization far better equipped to deal with criminals than she was. He was armed, for one thing, and she was not. She had just decided to follow Clarence Lawson when suddenly, with a snarl of rage, he whirled around toward her. Judy saw the gleam of a gun in his hand.

"You'd never use that!" she gasped, terrified.

He wasn't given time to answer. It was growing dark, but she could see a figure loom up behind him and whip the gun from his hand. Scuffling sounds followed. Judy heard a thud and then a splash.

"Peter!" she gasped. He had appeared from behind

her. "That—that was Lawson, the man you want—"

"You mean the man we've got. There's a good hiding place under the bridge," Peter continued as two policemen emerged with a dripping Lawson between them. "We walked into a trap all right, but it was set for a prisoner who can use one of those talking pillows I was telling you about."

CHAPTER XXV

Real Friends

"WHAT next?" asked Judy. Things were happening so fast she could scarcely keep track of them. "I thought you said—talking pillows—before all the excitement began. Oh, Peter, I was so afraid!"

"Judy, you're shivering! There's no need for you to be afraid now. Go back to the house," advised Peter. "I'll join you there in a few minutes."

"*She's* shivering! What about me?" Lawson snarled from between chattering teeth.

"You're lucky we didn't drown you," one of the police officers told him.

As he was led toward the barn where a police car was concealed, little pools of water dripped from his clothing and left a trail behind him in the melting snow. It had turned warm for January. Judy

161

had not shivered because of the cold. It was something else that sent chills through her. Things were too quiet. Usually, when a man was arrested, there were wailing sirens and a whole flock of police cars roaring in from all directions. Here there was nothing but an ominous silence.

The lights from the house looked friendly, but there wasn't a sound to prove that anyone was inside. Only Blackberry, on the porch now, yowled plaintively, asking to be let in.

Suddenly the door opened. Dr. Bolton was on his way out. He did have office hours and had waited only long enough to greet Judy. Her mother and Horace were just behind him. She heard Honey, somewhere in the background, saying in a loud stage whisper, "She's here, girls! All together!"

"Surprise!" came the chorus of voices as her friends rushed forward. Clarissa was with them. She hugged Judy fiercely. "It's good to see you," she said in a strange voice. "I told Mother and Father how I met you. Mother's here—" She indicated Blackberry's favorite chair where a motherly, gray-haired woman sat quietly rocking and smiling at the assembled guests.

"You haven't met Mrs. Valentine. Let me introduce you," Judy's mother began.

Horace gave her a secret sign that meant he knew and had come, not only as her brother but also as a reporter for the *Farringdon Daily Herald*. But, obviously, Mrs. Bolton had been kept in the dark.

Judy heard herself saying something polite instead of the questions that were tumbling over themselves in her mind wanting to be asked and answered.

Lois and Lorraine were there. Arthur Farringdon-Pett hovered protectively behind his sister and his recent bride. Judy's young neighbor, Holly Potter, said, "I like your friend Clarissa, Judy. I met her at school."

"Did you?" One question was answered. "I introduced her to Horace and Honey," Holly continued, and the answer came to another question. Judy felt more secure, suddenly, as she noticed another quiet guest. He was David Trent from the field office of the FBI.

"Everybody has been so friendly," Mrs. Valentine was telling him. "We've decided to join the little neighborhood church here until my husband has a call. You know, of course, that he is a minister of the gospel?"

"So I understand."

The gray-haired woman moved uncomfortably in her chair.

"I wonder what is keeping him. He promised to stop in and meet some of the young people. He has plans for a youth organization—"

"His plans, whatever they are, will never be carried out." Mr. Trent brought out his credentials, and the conversation ended abruptly just as Peter entered the room and took the woman firmly by the arm.

"You're G-men!" she gasped, looking from one of them to the other. She was not looking for a way to escape. She could see that there was none.

Afterwards, when Judy remembered the scene, the

one thing that stood out clearly in her mind was the fact that Blackberry had been insulted to see a stranger sitting in his chair and that he had jumped into it and settled himself to sleep before the excitement was fairly over.

Peter had mentioned the charge against the Lawsons. Judy's mother had gasped, "Kidnaping!" and Clarissa had said quietly, "I wasn't their daughter, Mrs. Bolton. I don't know what they would have done to me if I hadn't pretended. I led them here. I knew Judy would help me. You aren't supposed to tell peo-

ple what your husband does for a living, Judy, but I'm
so glad—glad that you let it slip out in the restaurant.
Did you get my letter?"

"We turned your letter over to the FBI," Judy told
her. "But who planned this welcoming party? I don't
understand—"

"I like parties. I like pretty girls, and I am especially fond of getting exclusive stories—"

"Horace! You did it. You perfect dear!" cried Judy,
throwing herself at her brother and giving him a re-
sounding kiss.

"Save the mush, Sis," he said, embarrassed.

"Well, it was a wonderful idea!" Judy exclaimed.
"You're all real friends!"

Clarissa's laugh rang out. "Am I real? Am I really
me? I've been Francine Dow and Clarissa Valentine,
but now I think I'd like to be just plain old Clar Boggs
and go back to West Virginia to my real folks. Pa's
a preacher just like I said, but we're real old hillbillies
for a fact, and I'm sick to death of pretending."

"Don't you want to be an actress any more?" asked
Judy.

"Maybe later when things are cleared up and I
understand—" Clarissa said.

"We'll clear them up right now," Judy interrupted. "Sit down, and we'll explain everything."

"While you're explaining I'll bring sandwiches and
coffee. There's cake, too. I still can't make tender pie
crust," Honey confessed, "but my cakes are good, and
Mother Bolton's sandwiches are delicious."

Mother Bolton? Judy looked at her brother. Was it that serious? Honey blushed and said hastily, "She's your mother, Judy, and you and I are sisters. She doesn't mind if I call her that. Sit down, everybody, and I'll pass the stuff around."

Judy ate half a sandwich and drank a full cup of coffee cooled with cream while she considered where to begin. It was a long story. But it really started in the restaurant.

"Clarissa, that cashier who tried to cheat you was arrested on some other charge. Peter told me about it," Judy said. "The police picked him up. It wasn't a federal offense, but the subliminal advertising that the golden hair wash people put on is a different matter." She explained to Clarissa about the messages that had been flashed on the screen too fast for their conscious minds to be aware of what was being suggested. "That's why you kept saying your hair was 'dull' and 'drab' and why we all rushed out and bought that shampoo when we didn't really want it."

"But I did want it," Clarissa protested. "I went back to the dressing room on purpose to get those two bottles I left there. I was going to come right back, but the first thing I knew I was being rushed into a costume and pushed out on the stage. Someone whispered, 'Watch the cards,' and I read the lines, but I was never so scared in my life. If my hair hadn't been covered up with that golden wig I don't think I could have played the part at all."

"You played it beautifully," Judy said.

Clarissa smiled and tilted her head.

"I could play Sleeping Beauty without a wig now. Did you notice the change?" she asked. "I used that golden hair wash."

CHAPTER XXVI

Talking Pillows

Judy had noticed a change in Clarissa's appearance. The shampoo had made her hair fluffy and bright.

"It's like mine," Honey said. "You sounded so strange over the telephone, Judy, when you asked me not to change the color of my hair. Why were you so afraid?"

"I like it the way it is. I guess that's why."

"Don't you like mine?" Clarissa asked plaintively. "I didn't use much of the shampoo. It hardly changed the color at all. It just brought out the golden highlights."

"It's lovely," Judy had to admit. "It isn't the product. It's the way they advertise it that's wrong. Peter calls 'hidden sell' advertisers thieves of the mind," she

169

continued, "but he says mind control can be used in another way."

"This is interesting," Horace said. "What is this other way our minds can be manipulated?"

"I—I'm not sure. Peter said something about talking pillows, but he may have been joking. I never heard of a pillow that talked."

"Maybe it works like a Mamma doll," Holly suggested, and everybody laughed.

"You tell us, Peter," urged Judy.

"The pillows I spoke of," Peter said, "are supposed to change a prisoner's outlook on life by what is called sleep teaching. They contain taped messages that are fed into his subconscious mind while he sleeps. 'You are filled with love and compassion' is one. For all I know Lawson's 'Do good and gain good' may be another. I don't know how well they work. A study is being made."

"What sort of a study?" asked Judy. "I wouldn't want anybody sleep-teaching me. I want to know what I'm learning."

Everybody agreed with Judy except Clarissa. She said she thought she'd like such a pillow if it would make her stop dreaming.

"I've had a terrible time," she confessed. "I haven't been able to draw a peaceful breath. I found out right away that this couple had planned to kidnap Francine Dow. They were so angry when they found out I'd substituted for her that I knew my only chance was pretending I cared for them and wanted them to be my mother and father. They thought they had my mind controlled, I guess, but they didn't. All the time I was awake I was making plans. The nights were the worst because I did have nightmares. Maybe they'll stop now that I know what caused them. I thought fear did. I was never so afraid."

"You aren't afraid any more, are you?" Honey asked anxiously.

"No," Clarissa replied with a deep sigh. "I'm with friends now—real friends. It's all over—all the fear and the pretending. I know I can act now, and I think I can take things a lot better, too. I mean little things like my brother's teasing."

"I used to find my brother's teasing pretty hard to take, but I teased him right back, and I guess there were times when it was harder on him than it was on me," Judy said with a glance toward Horace.

"I'll bet your brother wouldn't remove the glass from a silver mirror on purpose to make you think you didn't show. They tell lots of witch tales at home, and one of them is that if you look in a mirror and don't see your reflection, a witch has stolen the real you and you're a changeling. But now that I've really been stolen by a witch—That's what she is, Judy! That Mrs. Lawson or whatever her name is. She looks like somebody's mother, but she's nothing but an ugly old witch."

"There aren't any such things as witches," Judy laughed.

"I'll never believe it," Clarissa continued, "but I do know I'm no changeling. My brother was just trying to play a joke on me when he took out the glass and then put it back to prove he could see himself in the mirror all right. I'm going to tell him I know, and then he'll confess to it. I thought it all out, but I still can't understand why I didn't show on television. Everybody could see me when I took Francine Dow's place on Irene's show."

"A picture tube blew out," Judy started to explain. "That makes the picture close in—"

"Lawsy me!" exclaimed Clarissa, reverting to her mountain slang. "I let a little thing like that scare me into a faint?"

"You didn't let the big things scare you. Now that you know how brave you can be, I guess the little things won't bother you so much, will they?" Judy asked.

"They sure won't. I'll write to you all and tell you how I'm doing and I'll see you—I mean, maybe you'll see me on television one of these days."

The party had been a little tiring, Judy realized, after her guests had gone home. She picked up Blackberry and laid her head against his velvety black fur.

"Those prisoners can have their talking pillows," she said to Peter. "I prefer a pillow that purrs. For the rest of the evening we can just relax and watch television. Oh, how I wish we could watch Irene!"

Judy's wish came true a few weeks later. A postcard came with the good news. Or was it good? The card didn't say who Irene's sponsor would be. Surely Irene hadn't gone back on her decision! Would it be golden hair wash? Judy was almost afraid to watch.

Peter tuned in the set just in time for her to hear: ". . . bring you our own Golden Girl, Irene Meredith." And suddenly there was Irene as natural as though she had just stepped into the living room. And Irene was not alone on the stage. Little Judy was peeking out from behind her skirt like a small pixie. Judy couldn't believe it when she heard what they were about to sing.

"Oh, no! Irene can't sing that!" she exclaimed, turning to Peter.

"Listen!" Peter motioned for silence as the song began. Little Judy's small, piping voice could be heard on the second line. By the third line she was singing all by herself:

"I might sing and play like Mommy on TV or radio,

> *But I wouldn't do commercials,*
> *No, I wouldn't do commercials,*
> *No, I wouldn't do commercials*
> *And innerup the show—"*

It was Irene who interrupted, laughing.

"We just couldn't get that one word right. Judy Irene is only two and a half. I wouldn't interrupt the show either. But I do want to introduce a very good friend of ours, Clarissa Valentine! She will appear on this show regularly and will star again in *Sleeping Beauty* two weeks from tonight. Right now she has a message from our new sponsor."

The message was brief and in good taste. The sponsor turned out to be a nationally known manufacturer of cereal. Clarissa opened a box and poured out two servings of what she called crispy, crunchy nuggets of golden corn.

"That's how they're going to work it. Clarissa won't mind doing the commercial," Judy began, but again Peter held up his hand for silence. And suddenly, right there on the TV screen, was Judy's own little namesake doing a commercial and not even knowing it. For she sat down at a table opposite her mother and began eating the golden nuggets as if they were the tastiest things in the world.

"They're good, Mommy!" she said between mouthfuls.

"I like them, too. Why don't you try them?" Irene asked the TV audience as the commercial ended.

"I think I will," Judy answered as if Irene could hear her. Then she turned to Peter with shining eyes. "It was a joke!" she exclaimed. "They sang the song just for fun, and the studio audience enjoyed it. Did you hear the laughter? But it does prove truth can win if we stand up for what we believe. Oh, I'm so glad Irene talked to Mr. Lenz that day. She almost made the wrong decision."

"She didn't if those golden nuggets really are as good as the sponsor would have us believe," Peter said.

"Well, I'm sold on them," Judy declared, laughing. "And it didn't take any 'hidden sell' to do it. Just watching little Judy sitting there gobbling them up was enough. I'm going to buy a box tomorrow."

CPSIA information can be obtained at www.ICGtesting.com
Printed in the USA
241863LV00005B/26/P